C-4502   CAREER EXAMINATION SERIES

This is your
PASSBOOK for...

Park Supervisor II

Test Preparation Study Guide
Questions & Answers

COPYRIGHT NOTICE

This book is SOLELY intended for, is sold ONLY to, and its use is RESTRICTED to individual, bona fide applicants or candidates who qualify by virtue of having seriously filed applications for appropriate license, certificate, professional and/or promotional advancement, higher school matriculation, scholarship, or other legitimate requirements of education and/or governmental authorities.

This book is NOT intended for use, class instruction, tutoring, training, duplication, copying, reprinting, excerption, or adaptation, etc., by:

1) Other publishers
2) Proprietors and/or Instructors of "Coaching" and/or Preparatory Courses
3) Personnel and/or Training Divisions of commercial, industrial, and governmental organizations
4) Schools, colleges, or universities and/or their departments and staffs, including teachers and other personnel
5) Testing Agencies or Bureaus
6) Study groups which seek by the purchase of a single volume to copy and/or duplicate and/or adapt this material for use by the group as a whole without having purchased individual volumes for each of the members of the group
7) Et al.

Such persons would be in violation of appropriate Federal and State statutes.

PROVISION OF LICENSING AGREEMENTS – Recognized educational, commercial, industrial, and governmental institutions and organizations, and others legitimately engaged in educational pursuits, including training, testing, and measurement activities, may address request for a licensing agreement to the copyright owners, who will determine whether, and under what conditions, including fees and charges, the materials in this book may be used them. In other words, a licensing facility exists for the legitimate use of the material in this book on other than an individual basis. However, it is asseverated and affirmed here that the material in this book CANNOT be used without the receipt of the express permission of such a licensing agreement from the Publishers. Inquiries re licensing should be addressed to the company, attention rights and permissions department.

All rights reserved, including the right of reproduction in whole or in part, in any form or by any means, electronic or mechanical, including photocopying, recording, or by any information storage and retrieval system, without permission in writing from the Publisher.

Copyright © 2024 by
National Learning Corporation

212 Michael Drive, Syosset, NY 11791
(516) 921-8888 • www.passbooks.com
E-mail: info@passbooks.com

PASSBOOK® SERIES

THE *PASSBOOK® SERIES* has been created to prepare applicants and candidates for the ultimate academic battlefield – the examination room.

At some time in our lives, each and every one of us may be required to take an examination – for validation, matriculation, admission, qualification, registration, certification, or licensure.

Based on the assumption that every applicant or candidate has met the basic formal educational standards, has taken the required number of courses, and read the necessary texts, the *PASSBOOK® SERIES* furnishes the one special preparation which may assure passing with confidence, instead of failing with insecurity. Examination questions – together with answers – are furnished as the basic vehicle for study so that the mysteries of the examination and its compounding difficulties may be eliminated or diminished by a sure method.

This book is meant to help you pass your examination provided that you qualify and are serious in your objective.

The entire field is reviewed through the huge store of content information which is succinctly presented through a provocative and challenging approach – the question-and-answer method.

A climate of success is established by furnishing the correct answers at the end of each test.

You soon learn to recognize types of questions, forms of questions, and patterns of questioning. You may even begin to anticipate expected outcomes.

You perceive that many questions are repeated or adapted so that you can gain acute insights, which may enable you to score many sure points.

You learn how to confront new questions, or types of questions, and to attack them confidently and work out the correct answers.

You note objectives and emphases, and recognize pitfalls and dangers, so that you may make positive educational adjustments.

Moreover, you are kept fully informed in relation to new concepts, methods, practices, and directions in the field.

You discover that you are actually taking the examination all the time: you are preparing for the examination by "taking" an examination, not by reading extraneous and/or supererogatory textbooks.

In short, this PASSBOOK®, used directedly, should be an important factor in helping you to pass your test.

PARK SUPERVISOR II

DUTIES:
 Plans and supervises the operation and maintenance of a park and recreation complex or a group of small parks. Performs related duties as required.

SCOPE OF THE EXAMINATION:
The written test will be designed to test for knowledge, skills, and/or abilities in such areas as:
1. **Administrative Supervision** - These questions test for knowledge of the principles and practices involved in directing the activities of a large subordinate staff, including subordinate supervisors. Questions relate to the personal interactions between an upper level supervisor and his/her subordinate supervisors in the accomplishment of objectives. These questions cover such areas as assigning work to and coordinating the activities of several units, establishing and guiding staff development programs, evaluating the performance of subordinate supervisors, and maintaining relationships with other organizational sections.
2. **Educating and Interacting with the Public** - These questions test for knowledge of techniques used to interact effectively with individuals and/or community groups, to educate or inform them about topics of concern, to publicize or clarify agency programs or policies, to negotiate conflicts or resolve complaints, and to represent ones agency or program in a manner in keeping with good public relations practices. Questions may also cover interacting with others in cooperative efforts of public outreach or service.
3. **Maintenance of Buildings and Equipment** - These questions test for knowledge of the principles and practices involved in the overall maintenance, construction, and upkeep of the typical structures, buildings, and equipment found in park facilities; and may include such areas as proper maintenance and repair of buildings, roadways, trails, flood control and drainage structures. minor mechanical and electrical systems maintenance. and safe operating practices.
4. **Operation of Park Facilities** - These questions test for knowledge of the practices and procedures involved in operating park facilities and may include such typical areas as job safety, grounds and equipment maintenance, prioritizing work schedules, inspection and repair of park playgrounds, picnic areas, swimming facilities. public restrooms, hiking trails, and other park facilities, water and wastewater line repair, proper use of hand and power tools, revenue collection, customer and employee relations, and proper handling of emergency situations.
5. **Installation, Maintenance, and Repair of Recreation Areas** - These questions test for knowledge of the principles and practices involved in the installation, upkeep, maintenance and repair of park and recreation facilities, including such areas as picnic facilities, playgrounds, athletic and playing fields, trails and walkways, sanitary facilities, and lawn care and grounds maintenance.
6. **Preparing Written Material** - These questions test for the ability to present information clearly and accurately, and to organize paragraphs logically and comprehensibly. For some questions, you will be given information in two or three sentences followed by four restatements of the information. You must then choose the best version. For other questions, you will be given paragraphs with their sentences out of order. You must then choose. from four suggestions, the best order for the sentences.

HOW TO TAKE A TEST

I. YOU MUST PASS AN EXAMINATION

A. *WHAT EVERY CANDIDATE SHOULD KNOW*

Examination applicants often ask us for help in preparing for the written test. What can I study in advance? What kinds of questions will be asked? How will the test be given? How will the papers be graded?

As an applicant for a civil service examination, you may be wondering about some of these things. Our purpose here is to suggest effective methods of advance study and to describe civil service examinations.

Your chances for success on this examination can be increased if you know how to prepare. Those "pre-examination jitters" can be reduced if you know what to expect. You can even experience an adventure in good citizenship if you know why civil service exams are given.

B. *WHY ARE CIVIL SERVICE EXAMINATIONS GIVEN?*

Civil service examinations are important to you in two ways. As a citizen, you want public jobs filled by employees who know how to do their work. As a job seeker, you want a fair chance to compete for that job on an equal footing with other candidates. The best-known means of accomplishing this two-fold goal is the competitive examination.

Exams are widely publicized throughout the nation. They may be administered for jobs in federal, state, city, municipal, town or village governments or agencies.

Any citizen may apply, with some limitations, such as the age or residence of applicants. Your experience and education may be reviewed to see whether you meet the requirements for the particular examination. When these requirements exist, they are reasonable and applied consistently to all applicants. Thus, a competitive examination may cause you some uneasiness now, but it is your privilege and safeguard.

C. *HOW ARE CIVIL SERVICE EXAMS DEVELOPED?*

Examinations are carefully written by trained technicians who are specialists in the field known as "psychological measurement," in consultation with recognized authorities in the field of work that the test will cover. These experts recommend the subject matter areas or skills to be tested; only those knowledges or skills important to your success on the job are included. The most reliable books and source materials available are used as references. Together, the experts and technicians judge the difficulty level of the questions.

Test technicians know how to phrase questions so that the problem is clearly stated. Their ethics do not permit "trick" or "catch" questions. Questions may have been tried out on sample groups, or subjected to statistical analysis, to determine their usefulness.

Written tests are often used in combination with performance tests, ratings of training and experience, and oral interviews. All of these measures combine to form the best-known means of finding the right person for the right job.

II. HOW TO PASS THE WRITTEN TEST

A. NATURE OF THE EXAMINATION

To prepare intelligently for civil service examinations, you should know how they differ from school examinations you have taken. In school you were assigned certain definite pages to read or subjects to cover. The examination questions were quite detailed and usually emphasized memory. Civil service exams, on the other hand, try to discover your present ability to perform the duties of a position, plus your potentiality to learn these duties. In other words, a civil service exam attempts to predict how successful you will be. Questions cover such a broad area that they cannot be as minute and detailed as school exam questions.

In the public service similar kinds of work, or positions, are grouped together in one "class." This process is known as *position-classification*. All the positions in a class are paid according to the salary range for that class. One class title covers all of these positions, and they are all tested by the same examination.

B. FOUR BASIC STEPS

1) Study the announcement

How, then, can you know what subjects to study? Our best answer is: "Learn as much as possible about the class of positions for which you've applied." The exam will test the knowledge, skills and abilities needed to do the work.

Your most valuable source of information about the position you want is the official exam announcement. This announcement lists the training and experience qualifications. Check these standards and apply only if you come reasonably close to meeting them.

The brief description of the position in the examination announcement offers some clues to the subjects which will be tested. Think about the job itself. Review the duties in your mind. Can you perform them, or are there some in which you are rusty? Fill in the blank spots in your preparation.

Many jurisdictions preview the written test in the exam announcement by including a section called "Knowledge and Abilities Required," "Scope of the Examination," or some similar heading. Here you will find out specifically what fields will be tested.

2) Review your own background

Once you learn in general what the position is all about, and what you need to know to do the work, ask yourself which subjects you already know fairly well and which need improvement. You may wonder whether to concentrate on improving your strong areas or on building some background in your fields of weakness. When the announcement has specified "some knowledge" or "considerable knowledge," or has used adjectives like "beginning principles of…" or "advanced … methods," you can get a clue as to the number and difficulty of questions to be asked in any given field. More questions, and hence broader coverage, would be included for those subjects which are more important in the work. Now weigh your strengths and weaknesses against the job requirements and prepare accordingly.

3) Determine the level of the position

Another way to tell how intensively you should prepare is to understand the level of the job for which you are applying. Is it the entering level? In other words, is this the position in which beginners in a field of work are hired? Or is it an intermediate or advanced level? Sometimes this is indicated by such words as "Junior" or "Senior" in the class title. Other jurisdictions use Roman numerals to designate the level – Clerk I, Clerk II, for example. The word "Supervisor" sometimes appears in the title. If the level is not indicated by the title, check the description of duties. Will you be working under very close supervision, or will you have responsibility for independent decisions in this work?

4) Choose appropriate study materials

Now that you know the subjects to be examined and the relative amount of each subject to be covered, you can choose suitable study materials. For beginning level jobs, or even advanced ones, if you have a pronounced weakness in some aspect of your training, read a modern, standard textbook in that field. Be sure it is up to date and has general coverage. Such books are normally available at your library, and the librarian will be glad to help you locate one. For entry-level positions, questions of appropriate difficulty are chosen – neither highly advanced questions, nor those too simple. Such questions require careful thought but not advanced training.

If the position for which you are applying is technical or advanced, you will read more advanced, specialized material. If you are already familiar with the basic principles of your field, elementary textbooks would waste your time. Concentrate on advanced textbooks and technical periodicals. Think through the concepts and review difficult problems in your field.

These are all general sources. You can get more ideas on your own initiative, following these leads. For example, training manuals and publications of the government agency which employs workers in your field can be useful, particularly for technical and professional positions. A letter or visit to the government department involved may result in more specific study suggestions, and certainly will provide you with a more definite idea of the exact nature of the position you are seeking.

III. KINDS OF TESTS

Tests are used for purposes other than measuring knowledge and ability to perform specified duties. For some positions, it is equally important to test ability to make adjustments to new situations or to profit from training. In others, basic mental abilities not dependent on information are essential. Questions which test these things may not appear as pertinent to the duties of the position as those which test for knowledge and information. Yet they are often highly important parts of a fair examination. For very general questions, it is almost impossible to help you direct your study efforts. What we can do is to point out some of the more common of these general abilities needed in public service positions and describe some typical questions.

1) General information

Broad, general information has been found useful for predicting job success in some kinds of work. This is tested in a variety of ways, from vocabulary lists to questions about current events. Basic background in some field of work, such as sociology or economics, may be sampled in a group of questions. Often these are principles which have become familiar to most persons through exposure rather than through formal training. It is difficult to advise you how to study for these questions; being alert to the world around you is our best suggestion.

2) Verbal ability

An example of an ability needed in many positions is verbal or language ability. Verbal ability is, in brief, the ability to use and understand words. Vocabulary and grammar tests are typical measures of this ability. Reading comprehension or paragraph interpretation questions are common in many kinds of civil service tests. You are given a paragraph of written material and asked to find its central meaning.

3) Numerical ability

Number skills can be tested by the familiar arithmetic problem, by checking paired lists of numbers to see which are alike and which are different, or by interpreting charts and graphs. In the latter test, a graph may be printed in the test booklet which you are asked to use as the basis for answering questions.

4) Observation

A popular test for law-enforcement positions is the observation test. A picture is shown to you for several minutes, then taken away. Questions about the picture test your ability to observe both details and larger elements.

5) Following directions

In many positions in the public service, the employee must be able to carry out written instructions dependably and accurately. You may be given a chart with several columns, each column listing a variety of information. The questions require you to carry out directions involving the information given in the chart.

6) Skills and aptitudes

Performance tests effectively measure some manual skills and aptitudes. When the skill is one in which you are trained, such as typing or shorthand, you can practice. These tests are often very much like those given in business school or high school courses. For many of the other skills and aptitudes, however, no short-time preparation can be made. Skills and abilities natural to you or that you have developed throughout your lifetime are being tested.

Many of the general questions just described provide all the data needed to answer the questions and ask you to use your reasoning ability to find the answers. Your best preparation for these tests, as well as for tests of facts and ideas, is to be at your physical and mental best. You, no doubt, have your own methods of getting into an exam-taking mood and keeping "in shape." The next section lists some ideas on this subject.

IV. KINDS OF QUESTIONS

Only rarely is the "essay" question, which you answer in narrative form, used in civil service tests. Civil service tests are usually of the short-answer type. Full instructions for answering these questions will be given to you at the examination. But in case this is your first experience with short-answer questions and separate answer sheets, here is what you need to know:

1) Multiple-choice Questions

Most popular of the short-answer questions is the "multiple choice" or "best answer" question. It can be used, for example, to test for factual knowledge, ability to solve problems or judgment in meeting situations found at work.

A multiple-choice question is normally one of three types—
- It can begin with an incomplete statement followed by several possible endings. You are to find the one ending which *best* completes the statement, although some of the others may not be entirely wrong.
- It can also be a complete statement in the form of a question which is answered by choosing one of the statements listed.

- It can be in the form of a problem – again you select the best answer.

Here is an example of a multiple-choice question with a discussion which should give you some clues as to the method for choosing the right answer:

When an employee has a complaint about his assignment, the action which will *best* help him overcome his difficulty is to
   A. discuss his difficulty with his coworkers
   B. take the problem to the head of the organization
   C. take the problem to the person who gave him the assignment
   D. say nothing to anyone about his complaint

In answering this question, you should study each of the choices to find which is best. Consider choice "A" – Certainly an employee may discuss his complaint with fellow employees, but no change or improvement can result, and the complaint remains unresolved. Choice "B" is a poor choice since the head of the organization probably does not know what assignment you have been given, and taking your problem to him is known as "going over the head" of the supervisor. The supervisor, or person who made the assignment, is the person who can clarify it or correct any injustice. Choice "C" is, therefore, correct. To say nothing, as in choice "D," is unwise. Supervisors have and interest in knowing the problems employees are facing, and the employee is seeking a solution to his problem.

2) True/False Questions

The "true/false" or "right/wrong" form of question is sometimes used. Here a complete statement is given. Your job is to decide whether the statement is right or wrong.

SAMPLE: A roaming cell-phone call to a nearby city costs less than a non-roaming call to a distant city.

This statement is wrong, or false, since roaming calls are more expensive.
This is not a complete list of all possible question forms, although most of the others are variations of these common types. You will always get complete directions for answering questions. Be sure you understand *how* to mark your answers – ask questions until you do.

V. RECORDING YOUR ANSWERS

Computer terminals are used more and more today for many different kinds of exams.
For an examination with very few applicants, you may be told to record your answers in the test booklet itself. Separate answer sheets are much more common. If this separate answer sheet is to be scored by machine – and this is often the case – it is highly important that you mark your answers correctly in order to get credit.
An electronic scoring machine is often used in civil service offices because of the speed with which papers can be scored. Machine-scored answer sheets must be marked with a pencil, which will be given to you. This pencil has a high graphite content which responds to the electronic scoring machine. As a matter of fact, stray dots may register as answers, so do not let your pencil rest on the answer sheet while you are pondering the correct answer. Also, if your pencil lead breaks or is otherwise defective, ask for another.

Since the answer sheet will be dropped in a slot in the scoring machine, be careful not to bend the corners or get the paper crumpled.

The answer sheet normally has five vertical columns of numbers, with 30 numbers to a column. These numbers correspond to the question numbers in your test booklet. After each number, going across the page are four or five pairs of dotted lines. These short dotted lines have small letters or numbers above them. The first two pairs may also have a "T" or "F" above the letters. This indicates that the first two pairs only are to be used if the questions are of the true-false type. If the questions are multiple choice, disregard the "T" and "F" and pay attention only to the small letters or numbers.

Answer your questions in the manner of the sample that follows:

32. The largest city in the United States is
    A. Washington, D.C.
    B. New York City
    C. Chicago
    D. Detroit
    E. San Francisco

1) Choose the answer you think is best. (New York City is the largest, so "B" is correct.)
2) Find the row of dotted lines numbered the same as the question you are answering. (Find row number 32)
3) Find the pair of dotted lines corresponding to the answer. (Find the pair of lines under the mark "B.")
4) Make a solid black mark between the dotted lines.

VI. BEFORE THE TEST

Common sense will help you find procedures to follow to get ready for an examination. Too many of us, however, overlook these sensible measures. Indeed, nervousness and fatigue have been found to be the most serious reasons why applicants fail to do their best on civil service tests. Here is a list of reminders:

- Begin your preparation early – Don't wait until the last minute to go scurrying around for books and materials or to find out what the position is all about.
- Prepare continuously – An hour a night for a week is better than an all-night cram session. This has been definitely established. What is more, a night a week for a month will return better dividends than crowding your study into a shorter period of time.
- Locate the place of the exam – You have been sent a notice telling you when and where to report for the examination. If the location is in a different town or otherwise unfamiliar to you, it would be well to inquire the best route and learn something about the building.
- Relax the night before the test – Allow your mind to rest. Do not study at all that night. Plan some mild recreation or diversion; then go to bed early and get a good night's sleep.
- Get up early enough to make a leisurely trip to the place for the test – This way unforeseen events, traffic snarls, unfamiliar buildings, etc. will not upset you.
- Dress comfortably – A written test is not a fashion show. You will be known by number and not by name, so wear something comfortable.

- Leave excess paraphernalia at home – Shopping bags and odd bundles will get in your way. You need bring only the items mentioned in the official notice you received; usually everything you need is provided. Do not bring reference books to the exam. They will only confuse those last minutes and be taken away from you when in the test room.
- Arrive somewhat ahead of time – If because of transportation schedules you must get there very early, bring a newspaper or magazine to take your mind off yourself while waiting.
- Locate the examination room – When you have found the proper room, you will be directed to the seat or part of the room where you will sit. Sometimes you are given a sheet of instructions to read while you are waiting. Do not fill out any forms until you are told to do so; just read them and be prepared.
- Relax and prepare to listen to the instructions
- If you have any physical problem that may keep you from doing your best, be sure to tell the test administrator. If you are sick or in poor health, you really cannot do your best on the exam. You can come back and take the test some other time.

VII. AT THE TEST

The day of the test is here and you have the test booklet in your hand. The temptation to get going is very strong. Caution! There is more to success than knowing the right answers. You must know how to identify your papers and understand variations in the type of short-answer question used in this particular examination. Follow these suggestions for maximum results from your efforts:

1) Cooperate with the monitor

The test administrator has a duty to create a situation in which you can be as much at ease as possible. He will give instructions, tell you when to begin, check to see that you are marking your answer sheet correctly, and so on. He is not there to guard you, although he will see that your competitors do not take unfair advantage. He wants to help you do your best.

2) Listen to all instructions

Don't jump the gun! Wait until you understand all directions. In most civil service tests you get more time than you need to answer the questions. So don't be in a hurry. Read each word of instructions until you clearly understand the meaning. Study the examples, listen to all announcements and follow directions. Ask questions if you do not understand what to do.

3) Identify your papers

Civil service exams are usually identified by number only. You will be assigned a number; you must not put your name on your test papers. Be sure to copy your number correctly. Since more than one exam may be given, copy your exact examination title.

4) Plan your time

Unless you are told that a test is a "speed" or "rate of work" test, speed itself is usually not important. Time enough to answer all the questions will be provided, but this does not mean that you have all day. An overall time limit has been set. Divide the total time (in minutes) by the number of questions to determine the approximate time you have for each question.

5) Do not linger over difficult questions

If you come across a difficult question, mark it with a paper clip (useful to have along) and come back to it when you have been through the booklet. One caution if you do this – be sure to skip a number on your answer sheet as well. Check often to be sure that you have not lost your place and that you are marking in the row numbered the same as the question you are answering.

6) Read the questions

Be sure you know what the question asks! Many capable people are unsuccessful because they failed to *read* the questions correctly.

7) Answer all questions

Unless you have been instructed that a penalty will be deducted for incorrect answers, it is better to guess than to omit a question.

8) Speed tests

It is often better NOT to guess on speed tests. It has been found that on timed tests people are tempted to spend the last few seconds before time is called in marking answers at random – without even reading them – in the hope of picking up a few extra points. To discourage this practice, the instructions may warn you that your score will be "corrected" for guessing. That is, a penalty will be applied. The incorrect answers will be deducted from the correct ones, or some other penalty formula will be used.

9) Review your answers

If you finish before time is called, go back to the questions you guessed or omitted to give them further thought. Review other answers if you have time.

10) Return your test materials

If you are ready to leave before others have finished or time is called, take ALL your materials to the monitor and leave quietly. Never take any test material with you. The monitor can discover whose papers are not complete, and taking a test booklet may be grounds for disqualification.

VIII. EXAMINATION TECHNIQUES

1) Read the general instructions carefully. These are usually printed on the first page of the exam booklet. As a rule, these instructions refer to the timing of the examination; the fact that you should not start work until the signal and must stop work at a signal, etc. If there are any *special* instructions, such as a choice of questions to be answered, make sure that you note this instruction carefully.

2) When you are ready to start work on the examination, that is as soon as the signal has been given, read the instructions to each question booklet, underline any key words or phrases, such as *least, best, outline, describe* and the like. In this way you will tend to answer as requested rather than discover on reviewing your paper that you *listed without describing*, that you selected the *worst* choice rather than the *best* choice, etc.

3) If the examination is of the objective or multiple-choice type – that is, each question will also give a series of possible answers: A, B, C or D, and you are called upon to select the best answer and write the letter next to that answer on your answer paper – it is advisable to start answering each question in turn. There may be anywhere from 50 to 100 such questions in the three or four hours allotted and you can see how much time would be taken if you read through all the questions before beginning to answer any. Furthermore, if you come across a question or group of questions which you know would be difficult to answer, it would undoubtedly affect your handling of all the other questions.

4) If the examination is of the essay type and contains but a few questions, it is a moot point as to whether you should read all the questions before starting to answer any one. Of course, if you are given a choice – say five out of seven and the like – then it is essential to read all the questions so you can eliminate the two that are most difficult. If, however, you are asked to answer all the questions, there may be danger in trying to answer the easiest one first because you may find that you will spend too much time on it. The best technique is to answer the first question, then proceed to the second, etc.

5) Time your answers. Before the exam begins, write down the time it started, then add the time allowed for the examination and write down the time it must be completed, then divide the time available somewhat as follows:
    - If 3-1/2 hours are allowed, that would be 210 minutes. If you have 80 objective-type questions, that would be an average of 2-1/2 minutes per question. Allow yourself no more than 2 minutes per question, or a total of 160 minutes, which will permit about 50 minutes to review.
    - If for the time allotment of 210 minutes there are 7 essay questions to answer, that would average about 30 minutes a question. Give yourself only 25 minutes per question so that you have about 35 minutes to review.

6) The most important instruction is to *read each question* and make sure you know what is wanted. The second most important instruction is to *time yourself properly* so that you answer every question. The third most important instruction is to *answer every question*. Guess if you have to but include something for each question. Remember that you will receive no credit for a blank and will probably receive some credit if you write something in answer to an essay question. If you guess a letter – say "B" for a multiple-choice question – you may have guessed right. If you leave a blank as an answer to a multiple-choice question, the examiners may respect your feelings but it will not add a point to your score. Some exams may penalize you for wrong answers, so in such cases *only*, you may not want to guess unless you have some basis for your answer.

7) Suggestions
    a. Objective-type questions
        1. Examine the question booklet for proper sequence of pages and questions
        2. Read all instructions carefully
        3. Skip any question which seems too difficult; return to it after all other questions have been answered
        4. Apportion your time properly; do not spend too much time on any single question or group of questions

5. Note and underline key words – *all, most, fewest, least, best, worst, same, opposite*, etc.
6. Pay particular attention to negatives
7. Note unusual option, e.g., unduly long, short, complex, different or similar in content to the body of the question
8. Observe the use of "hedging" words – *probably, may, most likely*, etc.
9. Make sure that your answer is put next to the same number as the question
10. Do not second-guess unless you have good reason to believe the second answer is definitely more correct
11. Cross out original answer if you decide another answer is more accurate; do not erase until you are ready to hand your paper in
12. Answer all questions; guess unless instructed otherwise
13. Leave time for review

b. Essay questions
1. Read each question carefully
2. Determine exactly what is wanted. Underline key words or phrases.
3. Decide on outline or paragraph answer
4. Include many different points and elements unless asked to develop any one or two points or elements
5. Show impartiality by giving pros and cons unless directed to select one side only
6. Make and write down any assumptions you find necessary to answer the questions
7. Watch your English, grammar, punctuation and choice of words
8. Time your answers; don't crowd material

8) Answering the essay question

Most essay questions can be answered by framing the specific response around several key words or ideas. Here are a few such key words or ideas:

M's: manpower, materials, methods, money, management
P's: purpose, program, policy, plan, procedure, practice, problems, pitfalls, personnel, public relations

a. Six basic steps in handling problems:
1. Preliminary plan and background development
2. Collect information, data and facts
3. Analyze and interpret information, data and facts
4. Analyze and develop solutions as well as make recommendations
5. Prepare report and sell recommendations
6. Install recommendations and follow up effectiveness

b. Pitfalls to avoid
1. *Taking things for granted* – A statement of the situation does not necessarily imply that each of the elements is necessarily true; for example, a complaint may be invalid and biased so that all that can be taken for granted is that a complaint has been registered

2. *Considering only one side of a situation* – Wherever possible, indicate several alternatives and then point out the reasons you selected the best one
3. *Failing to indicate follow up* – Whenever your answer indicates action on your part, make certain that you will take proper follow-up action to see how successful your recommendations, procedures or actions turn out to be
4. *Taking too long in answering any single question* – Remember to time your answers properly

IX. AFTER THE TEST

Scoring procedures differ in detail among civil service jurisdictions although the general principles are the same. Whether the papers are hand-scored or graded by machine we have described, they are nearly always graded by number. That is, the person who marks the paper knows only the number – never the name – of the applicant. Not until all the papers have been graded will they be matched with names. If other tests, such as training and experience or oral interview ratings have been given, scores will be combined. Different parts of the examination usually have different weights. For example, the written test might count 60 percent of the final grade, and a rating of training and experience 40 percent. In many jurisdictions, veterans will have a certain number of points added to their grades.

After the final grade has been determined, the names are placed in grade order and an eligible list is established. There are various methods for resolving ties between those who get the same final grade – probably the most common is to place first the name of the person whose application was received first. Job offers are made from the eligible list in the order the names appear on it. You will be notified of your grade and your rank as soon as all these computations have been made. This will be done as rapidly as possible.

People who are found to meet the requirements in the announcement are called "eligibles." Their names are put on a list of eligible candidates. An eligible's chances of getting a job depend on how high he stands on this list and how fast agencies are filling jobs from the list.

When a job is to be filled from a list of eligibles, the agency asks for the names of people on the list of eligibles for that job. When the civil service commission receives this request, it sends to the agency the names of the three people highest on this list. Or, if the job to be filled has specialized requirements, the office sends the agency the names of the top three persons who meet these requirements from the general list.

The appointing officer makes a choice from among the three people whose names were sent to him. If the selected person accepts the appointment, the names of the others are put back on the list to be considered for future openings.

That is the rule in hiring from all kinds of eligible lists, whether they are for typist, carpenter, chemist, or something else. For every vacancy, the appointing officer has his choice of any one of the top three eligibles on the list. This explains why the person whose name is on top of the list sometimes does not get an appointment when some of the persons lower on the list do. If the appointing officer chooses the second or third eligible, the No. 1 eligible does not get a job at once, but stays on the list until he is appointed or the list is terminated.

X. HOW TO PASS THE INTERVIEW TEST

The examination for which you applied requires an oral interview test. You have already taken the written test and you are now being called for the interview test – the final part of the formal examination.

You may think that it is not possible to prepare for an interview test and that there are no procedures to follow during an interview. Our purpose is to point out some things you can do in advance that will help you and some good rules to follow and pitfalls to avoid while you are being interviewed.

What is an interview supposed to test?

The written examination is designed to test the technical knowledge and competence of the candidate; the oral is designed to evaluate intangible qualities, not readily measured otherwise, and to establish a list showing the relative fitness of each candidate – as measured against his competitors – for the position sought. Scoring is not on the basis of "right" and "wrong," but on a sliding scale of values ranging from "not passable" to "outstanding." As a matter of fact, it is possible to achieve a relatively low score without a single "incorrect" answer because of evident weakness in the qualities being measured.

Occasionally, an examination may consist entirely of an oral test – either an individual or a group oral. In such cases, information is sought concerning the technical knowledges and abilities of the candidate, since there has been no written examination for this purpose. More commonly, however, an oral test is used to supplement a written examination.

Who conducts interviews?

The composition of oral boards varies among different jurisdictions. In nearly all, a representative of the personnel department serves as chairman. One of the members of the board may be a representative of the department in which the candidate would work. In some cases, "outside experts" are used, and, frequently, a businessman or some other representative of the general public is asked to serve. Labor and management or other special groups may be represented. The aim is to secure the services of experts in the appropriate field.

However the board is composed, it is a good idea (and not at all improper or unethical) to ascertain in advance of the interview who the members are and what groups they represent. When you are introduced to them, you will have some idea of their backgrounds and interests, and at least you will not stutter and stammer over their names.

What should be done before the interview?

While knowledge about the board members is useful and takes some of the surprise element out of the interview, there is other preparation which is more substantive. It *is* possible to prepare for an oral interview – in several ways:

1) Keep a copy of your application and review it carefully before the interview

This may be the only document before the oral board, and the starting point of the interview. Know what education and experience you have listed there, and the sequence and dates of all of it. Sometimes the board will ask you to review the highlights of your experience for them; you should not have to hem and haw doing it.

2) Study the class specification and the examination announcement

Usually, the oral board has one or both of these to guide them. The qualities, characteristics or knowledges required by the position sought are stated in these documents. They offer valuable clues as to the nature of the oral interview. For example, if the job involves supervisory responsibilities, the announcement will usually indicate that knowledge of modern supervisory methods and the qualifications of the candidate as a supervisor will be tested. If so, you can expect such questions, frequently in the form of a hypothetical situation which you are expected to solve. NEVER go into an oral without knowledge of the duties and responsibilities of the job you seek.

3) Think through each qualification required

Try to visualize the kind of questions you would ask if you were a board member. How well could you answer them? Try especially to appraise your own knowledge and background in each area, *measured against the job sought*, and identify any areas in which you are weak. Be critical and realistic – do not flatter yourself.

4) Do some general reading in areas in which you feel you may be weak

For example, if the job involves supervision and your past experience has NOT, some general reading in supervisory methods and practices, particularly in the field of human relations, might be useful. Do NOT study agency procedures or detailed manuals. The oral board will be testing your understanding and capacity, not your memory.

5) Get a good night's sleep and watch your general health and mental attitude

You will want a clear head at the interview. Take care of a cold or any other minor ailment, and of course, no hangovers.

What should be done on the day of the interview?

Now comes the day of the interview itself. Give yourself plenty of time to get there. Plan to arrive somewhat ahead of the scheduled time, particularly if your appointment is in the fore part of the day. If a previous candidate fails to appear, the board might be ready for you a bit early. By early afternoon an oral board is almost invariably behind schedule if there are many candidates, and you may have to wait. Take along a book or magazine to read, or your application to review, but leave any extraneous material in the waiting room when you go in for your interview. In any event, relax and compose yourself.

The matter of dress is important. The board is forming impressions about you – from your experience, your manners, your attitude, and your appearance. Give your personal appearance careful attention. Dress your best, but not your flashiest. Choose conservative, appropriate clothing, and be sure it is immaculate. This is a business interview, and your appearance should indicate that you regard it as such. Besides, being well groomed and properly dressed will help boost your confidence.

Sooner or later, someone will call your name and escort you into the interview room. *This is it.* From here on you are on your own. It is too late for any more preparation. But remember, you asked for this opportunity to prove your fitness, and you are here because your request was granted.

What happens when you go in?

The usual sequence of events will be as follows: The clerk (who is often the board stenographer) will introduce you to the chairman of the oral board, who will introduce you to the other members of the board. Acknowledge the introductions before you sit down. Do not be surprised if you find a microphone facing you or a stenotypist sitting by. Oral interviews are usually recorded in the event of an appeal or other review.

Usually the chairman of the board will open the interview by reviewing the highlights of your education and work experience from your application – primarily for the benefit of the other members of the board, as well as to get the material into the record. Do not interrupt or comment unless there is an error or significant misinterpretation; if that is the case, do not hesitate. But do not quibble about insignificant matters. Also, he will usually ask you some question about your education, experience or your present job – partly to get you to start talking and to establish the interviewing "rapport." He may start the actual questioning, or turn it over to one of the other members. Frequently, each member undertakes the questioning on a particular area, one in which he is perhaps most competent, so you can expect each member to participate in the examination. Because time is limited, you may also expect some rather abrupt switches in the direction the questioning takes, so do not be upset by it. Normally, a board member will not pursue a single line of questioning unless he discovers a particular strength or weakness.

After each member has participated, the chairman will usually ask whether any member has any further questions, then will ask you if you have anything you wish to add. Unless you are expecting this question, it may floor you. Worse, it may start you off on an extended, extemporaneous speech. The board is not usually seeking more information. The question is principally to offer you a last opportunity to present further qualifications or to indicate that you have nothing to add. So, if you feel that a significant qualification or characteristic has been overlooked, it is proper to point it out in a sentence or so. Do not compliment the board on the thoroughness of their examination – they have been sketchy, and you know it. If you wish, merely say, "No thank you, I have nothing further to add." This is a point where you can "talk yourself out" of a good impression or fail to present an important bit of information. Remember, *you close the interview yourself.*

The chairman will then say, "That is all, Mr. _____, thank you." Do not be startled; the interview is over, and quicker than you think. Thank him, gather your belongings and take your leave. Save your sigh of relief for the other side of the door.

How to put your best foot forward

Throughout this entire process, you may feel that the board individually and collectively is trying to pierce your defenses, seek out your hidden weaknesses and embarrass and confuse you. Actually, this is not true. They are obliged to make an appraisal of your qualifications for the job you are seeking, and they want to see you in your best light. Remember, they must interview all candidates and a non-cooperative candidate may become a failure in spite of their best efforts to bring out his qualifications. Here are 15 suggestions that will help you:

1) Be natural – Keep your attitude confident, not cocky

If you are not confident that you can do the job, do not expect the board to be. Do not apologize for your weaknesses, try to bring out your strong points. The board is interested in a positive, not negative, presentation. Cockiness will antagonize any board member and make him wonder if you are covering up a weakness by a false show of strength.

2) Get comfortable, but don't lounge or sprawl

Sit erectly but not stiffly. A careless posture may lead the board to conclude that you are careless in other things, or at least that you are not impressed by the importance of the occasion. Either conclusion is natural, even if incorrect. Do not fuss with your clothing, a pencil or an ashtray. Your hands may occasionally be useful to emphasize a point; do not let them become a point of distraction.

3) Do not wisecrack or make small talk

This is a serious situation, and your attitude should show that you consider it as such. Further, the time of the board is limited – they do not want to waste it, and neither should you.

4) Do not exaggerate your experience or abilities

In the first place, from information in the application or other interviews and sources, the board may know more about you than you think. Secondly, you probably will not get away with it. An experienced board is rather adept at spotting such a situation, so do not take the chance.

5) If you know a board member, do not make a point of it, yet do not hide it

Certainly you are not fooling him, and probably not the other members of the board. Do not try to take advantage of your acquaintanceship – it will probably do you little good.

6) Do not dominate the interview

Let the board do that. They will give you the clues – do not assume that you have to do all the talking. Realize that the board has a number of questions to ask you, and do not try to take up all the interview time by showing off your extensive knowledge of the answer to the first one.

7) Be attentive

You only have 20 minutes or so, and you should keep your attention at its sharpest throughout. When a member is addressing a problem or question to you, give him your undivided attention. Address your reply principally to him, but do not exclude the other board members.

8) Do not interrupt

A board member may be stating a problem for you to analyze. He will ask you a question when the time comes. Let him state the problem, and wait for the question.

9) Make sure you understand the question

Do not try to answer until you are sure what the question is. If it is not clear, restate it in your own words or ask the board member to clarify it for you. However, do not haggle about minor elements.

10) Reply promptly but not hastily

A common entry on oral board rating sheets is "candidate responded readily," or "candidate hesitated in replies." Respond as promptly and quickly as you can, but do not jump to a hasty, ill-considered answer.

11) Do not be peremptory in your answers

A brief answer is proper – but do not fire your answer back. That is a losing game from your point of view. The board member can probably ask questions much faster than you can answer them.

12) Do not try to create the answer you think the board member wants

He is interested in what kind of mind you have and how it works – not in playing games. Furthermore, he can usually spot this practice and will actually grade you down on it.

13) Do not switch sides in your reply merely to agree with a board member

Frequently, a member will take a contrary position merely to draw you out and to see if you are willing and able to defend your point of view. Do not start a debate, yet do not surrender a good position. If a position is worth taking, it is worth defending.

14) Do not be afraid to admit an error in judgment if you are shown to be wrong

The board knows that you are forced to reply without any opportunity for careful consideration. Your answer may be demonstrably wrong. If so, admit it and get on with the interview.

15) Do not dwell at length on your present job

The opening question may relate to your present assignment. Answer the question but do not go into an extended discussion. You are being examined for a *new* job, not your present one. As a matter of fact, try to phrase ALL your answers in terms of the job for which you are being examined.

Basis of Rating

Probably you will forget most of these "do's" and "don'ts" when you walk into the oral interview room. Even remembering them all will not ensure you a passing grade. Perhaps you did not have the qualifications in the first place. But remembering them will help you to put your best foot forward, without treading on the toes of the board members.

Rumor and popular opinion to the contrary notwithstanding, an oral board wants you to make the best appearance possible. They know you are under pressure – but they also want to see how you respond to it as a guide to what your reaction would be under the pressures of the job you seek. They will be influenced by the degree of poise you display, the personal traits you show and the manner in which you respond.

ABOUT THIS BOOK

This book contains tests divided into Examination Sections. Go through each test, answering every question in the margin. We have also attached a sample answer sheet at the back of the book that can be removed and used. At the end of each test look at the answer key and check your answers. On the ones you got wrong, look at the right answer choice and learn. Do not fill in the answers first. Do not memorize the questions and answers, but understand the answer and principles involved. On your test, the questions will likely be different from the samples. Questions are changed and new ones added. If you understand these past questions you should have success with any changes that arise. Tests may consist of several types of questions. We have additional books on each subject should more study be advisable or necessary for you. Finally, the more you study, the better prepared you will be. This book is intended to be the last thing you study before you walk into the examination room. Prior study of relevant texts is also recommended. NLC publishes some of these in our Fundamental Series. Knowledge and good sense are important factors in passing your exam. Good luck also helps. So now study this Passbook, absorb the material contained within and take that knowledge into the examination. Then do your best to pass that exam.

EXAMINATION SECTION

EXAMINATION SECTION
TEST 1

DIRECTIONS: Each question or incomplete statement is followed by several suggested answers or completions. Select the one that BEST answers the question or completes the statement. *PRINT THE LETTER OF THE CORRECT ANSWER IN THE SPACE AT THE RIGHT.*

1. A specialist is meeting with a panel of local community leaders to determine their perceptions about the effectiveness of a recent outreach program. The leaders seem unresponsive to the specialist's questions, looking at the floor or each other without directly answering the specialist's questions.
One strategy that might work to elicit the desired information would be to
   A. try to discern the hidden meaning of their silence
   B. adopt a mildly confrontational tone and remind them of what's at stake in the community
   C. keep asking open-ended questions and wait patiently for responses
   D. tell them to come back when they're ready to tell you their opinions

1.____

2. Each of the following statements about maintaining a community's attention is true, EXCEPT:
   A. The more challenging it is to pay attention to a message, the more likely it is that it will be attended to
   B. Listeners will be more motivated to pay attention if a speech is personally meaningful
   C. People will be more likely to attend if a speaker pauses to suggest natural transitions in a speech
   D. Listeners will attend to messages that stand out

2.____

3. Each of the following is a key strategy to integrative bargaining among community members in conflict, EXCEPT
   A. focusing on positions, rather than interests
   B. separating the people from the problem
   C. aiming for an outcome based on an objectively identified standard
   D. using active listening skills, such as rephrasing and questioning

3.____

4. Which of the following is NOT one of the major variables to take into account when considering a community needs assessment?
   A. State of program development   B. Resources available
   C. Demographics   D. Community attitudes

4.____

5. Which of the following groups would probably be formed specifically for, or be involved in, the purpose of addressing a specific unmet community need?
   A. An existing consumer group
   B. A council of community representatives
   C. A committee
   D. An existing community organization

5.____

6. If a public outreach campaign designed to mobilize a community fails, the MOST likely reason for this failure is that the campaign
   A. was not specific about what it wanted people to do
   B. was overly serious and did not appeal to people's sense of humor
   C. offered no incentive for the audience to make a change
   D. did not use language that appealed to the audience's emotions

7. Nationwide, the rate of involvement of elderly people in community-based programs demonstrates that they are
   A. under-served when compared to other age groups
   B. served at about the same rate as other age groups
   C. over-served when compared to other age groups
   D. hardly served at all

8. In projecting the likelihood of an education program's success, a domestic violence specialist identifies every single event that must occur to complete the project. The specialist then arranges these events in sequential order and allocates time requirements for each. Finally, the total time is calculated and a model showing all their events and timelines is charted.
   The specialist has used
   A. a PERT chart   B. a simulation
   C. a Markov model   D. the critical path method

9. When working with members of a predominantly African-American community, specialists from other cultural backgrounds should be aware that African-Americans tend to express thoughts and feelings through descriptions of
   A. physically tangible sensations   B. problems to be analyzed
   C. corresponding analogies   D. spiritual issues

10. Local nonprofessionals should be considered useful to a specialist who is looking to undertake a community outreach or educational initiative.
    Which of the following is LEAST likely to be a characteristic or role demonstrated by these community members?
    A. Undertaking support functions at the agency
    B. Serving as a communication channel between the agency and clients
    C. Encouraging greater agency acceptance and credibility within the community
    D. Helping the agency to accomplish meaningful change

11. In working with Native American groups or clients, it is important to recognize that the GREATEST health problem facing their communities today is
    A. domestic violence   B. depression and suicide
    C. alcoholism   D. tuberculosis

12. A specialist is facilitating a cooperative conflict resolution session between community members who have different opinions about what kinds of intervention services should be offered by the local adult protective services agency.
    Which of the following is NOT a guideline that should be followed in this process?
    A. Early in the negotiations, ask each party to name the issues on which they will positively not yield.
    B. Try to get the parties to view the issue from other points of view, beside the two or three conflicting ones.
    C. Have each side volunteer what it would be willing to do to resolve the conflict.
    D. At the end of the session, draw up a formal agreement with agreed-upon actions for both parties.

12.____

13. A specialist wants to evaluate the effectiveness of a local women's shelter. The shelter has suffered from lax participation, given the number of women who have been abused in the surrounding area. The specialist wants to speak with the women in the community who did not follow up on referrals to the shelter, and begins by visiting some of these women. After gaining the trust of these women, the specialist asks for the names of women they know who might be in need of help with a domestic violence situation.
    The specialist's approach in this case is _____ sampling.
    A. maximum variation   B. snowball
    C. convenience   D. typical case

13.____

14. When it comes to perceiving messages, people typically DON'T
    A. tend to simplify causal connections and sometimes even seek a single cause to explain what may be a highly complex effect
    B. tend to perceive messages independently of a categorical framework, especially if the message may be distorted by such an interpretation
    C. have a predisposition toward accepting any pattern that a speaker offers to explain seemingly unconnected facts
    D. tend to interpret things in the way they are viewed by their reference group

14.____

15. The elder members of Native American communities, regardless of kinship, are MOST commonly referred to as
    A. the ancients   B. father or mother
    C. grandfather or grandmother D. chiefs

15.____

16. Each of the following is typically an objective of community mobilization, EXCEPT:
    A. To convince existing community resources to alter their services or work together to address an unmet need
    B. To gather and distribute information to consumers and agencies about unmet needs

16.____

C. To publicize existing community resources and make them more accessible
D. To bring an unmet community need to public attention in order to achieve acceptance of and support for fulfilling the need

17. Research in community outreach shows that women often build friendships through shared positive feelings, whereas men often build friendships through
    A. metacommunication   B. catharsis
    C. impression management D. shared activities

18. Typically, the FIRST step in a community-needs assessment is to
    A. identify community's strengths
    B. explore the nature of the neighborhood
    C. get to know the area and its residents
    D. talk to people in the community

19. Most public relations experts agree that _____ exposure(s) to a message is the minimum just to get the message noticed. If the aim of a public outreach campaign is action or a change in behavior, the agency budget must plan for more exposures.
    A. one   B. two   C. three   D. four

20. In the program development/community liaison model of community work and public outreach, the PRIMARY constituency is considered to be
    A. community representatives and the service agency board or administrators
    B. elected officials, social agencies, and interagency organizations
    C. marginalized or oppressed population groups in a city or region
    D. residents of a neighborhood, parish or rural county

21. Social or interpersonal problems in many African-American communities have their roots in
    A. personality deficits   B. unresolved family conflicts
    C. poor communication   D. external stressors

22. A public outreach campaign should
    I. focus on short-term, measurable goals, rather than ultimate outcomes
    II. try to alter entrenched attitudes within a short time, with powerfully worded messages
    III. proceed in steps or phases, each of which lays out a mechanism that leads to the desired effect
    IV. ignore causes that led to a problem, and instead focus on solutions

    The CORRECT answer is:
    A. I and II   B. II and III   C. III only   D. I, II, III and IV

23. Research findings indicate that in listing preferences for helping professional attributes, individuals from culturally diverse groups are MOST likely to consider _____ as more important than _____.
    A. personality similarity; either race/ethnic similarity or attitude similarity
    B. therapist experience; any kind of similarity
    C. race/ethnic similarity; attitude similarity
    D. attitude similarity; race/ethnic similarity

24. Each of the following is considered to be an objective of community organization EXCEPT
    A. effecting changes in the distribution of decision-making power
    B. helping people develop and strengthen the traits of self-direction and cooperation
    C. effecting and maintaining the balance between needs and resources in a community
    D. helping people deal with their problems by developing alternative behaviors

25. A specialist is helping the adult protective services agency to design a public outreach campaign. The topic to be addressed is complex, public understanding is low, and most professionals at the agency feel that having more complete information might change the opinions of community members. Which method of pre-campaign research is probably MOST appropriate?
    A. Deliberative polling
    B. Attitude scales
    C. Surveys or questionnaires
    D. Focus groups

KEY (CORRECT ANSWERS)

1.	C	11.	C
2.	A	12.	A
3.	A	13.	B
4.	C	14.	B
5.	C	15.	C
6.	A	16.	B
7.	A	17.	D
8.	D	18.	B
9.	C	19.	C
10.	A	20.	A

21.	D
22.	C
23.	D
24.	D
25.	A

TEST 2

DIRECTIONS: Each question or incomplete statement is followed by several suggested answers or completions. Select the one that BEST answers the question or completes the statement. *PRINT THE LETTER OF THE CORRECT ANSWER IN THE SPACE AT THE RIGHT.*

1. A specialist has been called in to resolve a dispute between two community leaders who have been arguing about the level of service needed within the community. The discussion has been going on for several hours when the specialist arrives, and both people seem to be upset.
After calming the two down and getting each of them to agree on a statement of the problem, the specialist should ask each person to
   A. summarize his or her argument in three main points
   B. explain why he or she became so upset
   C. clearly state, in objective terms, the position of the other in a form that meets with the other's approval
   D. identify the best alternative outcome, other than their presumed ideal

1._____

2. In evaluating the impact of a public outreach campaign, the _____ model can be used early in the campaign to address first impressions.
   A. exposure or advertising
   B. expert interview
   C. impact monitoring or process
   D. experimental or quasi-experimental

2._____

3. When trying to motivate an older population to take action on a community problem, it is helpful to remember that older people
   A. are more self-reliant in their decision-making than other members of the same family
   B. often need more time to decide than younger people
   C. are more likely than younger people to view community problems self-referentially
   D. tend to take a pragmatic, rather than philosophical, view of life

3._____

4. The method of group or community decision-making that is normally MOST time-consuming is
   A. majority opinion   B. consensus
   C. expert opinion   D. authority rule

4._____

5. A local adult protective services agency has identified one of the goals of its recent public outreach campaign to be the mobilization of activists.
The campaign should probably
   A. target neutral audiences
   B. home in on supporters
   C. stick to purely factual information
   D. try to persuade community fence-sitters

5._____

6. Research of Native American youths' perceptions of family concerns for their well-being has generally found that these youths
    A. have a high degree of uncertainty about their families' feelings toward them
    B. believe their families don't care about them
    C. believe that their mothers care a great deal about them, but their fathers don't
    D. believe their families care a great deal about them

7. A domestic violence specialist is developing a new outreach program for the local community. The specialist has defined the target problem, set program goals, and planned the actions that will take place as a result of the program. Most likely, the next step will be to
    A. evaluate the resources available to achieve program goals
    B. define and sequence the steps that will be taken to achieve program goals
    C. determine how the program will be evaluated
    D. decide how the program will operate

8. Elder: *I'm so glad to have someone to talk to, someone who really understands my problem.*
   Specialist: *It is nice to be able to talk to someone who will listen.*
   Elder: *That's for sure.*
   In the above exchange, what listening skill is evident in the underlined statement?
    A. Verbatim response
    B. Paraphrasing
    C. Advising
    D. Evaluation

9. Which of the following activities is involved in the specialist's task of mobilizing?
    A. Meeting individuals in the community with problems and assisting them in finding help
    B. Identifying unmet community needs
    C. Speaking out against an unjust policy or procedure
    D. Developing new services or linking presently available services to meet community needs

10. The preliminary research associated with a public outreach campaign should FIRST be aimed at determining
    A. the budget
    B. the message's ultimate audience
    C. what media to use
    D. the short-term behavioral goals of the campaign

11. A specialist in a low-income community wants to plan programs that will deal with the influence of unemployment on domestic disturbances. The specialist needs to know not only how many unemployed people are in the community now, but also how many people will be unemployed at any particular tie in the future, and how those numbers will vary given certain conditions.

Probably the BEST way to trace employment rates over time and within differing conditions is through the use of
A. the critical path
B. linear programming
C. difference equations
D. the Markov model

12. Generally, public outreach programs—whatever their stated goal—should
   I. create a sense of urgency about a problem
   II. decline to identify opponents of the issue or idea
   III. propose concrete, easily understandable solutions
   IV. urge a specific action

   The CORRECT answer is:
   A. I only   B. I, III and IV   C. II and III   D. I, II, III and IV

13. Which of the following methods of community needs assessment relies to the GREATEST degree on existing public records?
   A. Social indicators
   B. Field study
   C. Rates under treatment
   D. Key informant

14. During an interview with a Native American client, a specialist is careful to maintain close and nearly constant eye contact.
   The client is MOST likely to interpret this as a(n)
   A. show of high concern
   B. sign of disrespect
   C. uncomfortable assumption of intimacy
   D. attempt to intimidate

15. The BEST strategy for addressing an audience that is known to be captive, or even hostile, is to
   A. refer to experiences in common
   B. flatter the audience
   C. joke about things in or near the audience
   D. plead for fairness

16. Integrative conflict resolution is characterized by
   A. an overriding concern to maximize joint outcomes
   B. one side's interests opposing the other's
   C. a fixed and limited amount of resources to be divided, so that the more one group gets, the less another gets
   D. manipulation and withholding information as negotiation strategies

17. A specialist wants to learn how to interact with the members of a largely Latino community in a more culturally sensitive way.
   Which of the following is NOT a guideline for interacting with members of a Latino community?
   A. Efforts to foster independence and self-reliance may be interpreted by many Latinos as a lack of concern for others.
   B. Efforts to deal one-on-one with an adolescent client may serve to alienate the parents, especially the mother.

C. A nonverbal gesture, such as lowering the eyes, is interpreted by many Latinos as a sign of respect and deference to authority.
D. In much of Latino culture, the focus of control for problems tends to be much more external than internal.

18. Each of the following is a supporting assumption of community organization, EXCEPT:
    A. Democracy requires cooperative participation.
    B. In order for communities to change, it is necessary for each individual in the community to be willing to change.
    C. Communities often need help with organization and planning.
    D. Holistic approaches work better than fragmented or ad-hoc programs.

18.____

19. Helping professionals often have difficulty to bring community resources together to fulfill unmet community needs.
    Which of the following is NOT usually a reason for this?
    A. Some community groups resist assistance when it is offered.
    B. Few community groups make their needs known.
    C. Community resources frequently change the type of services they offer.
    D. Often, community resources prefer to work alone.

19.____

20. When dealing with groups or populations of elderly clients, specialists should be mindful that about _____ of the nation's elderly suffer from mental health problems.
    A. a tenth   B. a quarter   C. a third   D. half

20.____

21. In an African-American community, a specialist from another culture should recognize that church participation, for most African-Americans, is viewed as a
    A. method for maintaining control and communicating competency
    B. way of depersonalizing problems or troubles
    C. way to divert attention away from problems
    D. means of cathartic emotional release

21.____

22. Adult protective service programs supported by state statutes protect elderly people from abuse and neglect under the doctrine of
    A. parens patriae   B. habeas corpus
    C. in loco parentis   D. volenti non fit injuria

22.____

23. In terms of public outreach, which of the following statements about an audience is NOT generally true?
    A. The more heterogeneous the audience, the more necessary it will be to use specific examples and appeals to certain types of people.
    B. The smaller the audience, the more likely that its members will share assumptions and values.
    C. When the speaker does not know the status of an audience, it is best to assume that they are captive rather than voluntary.
    D. The larger an audience, the more formal a presentation is likely to be.

23.____

24. A specialist often spends time in the places frequented by community residents. She listens carefully to what residents seem most concerned about, and engages many in conversations, asking them how they see the problems in the community. During these conversations, she makes mental notes about whether the statements of the problems are the same things that are mentioned in their conversations. From these conversations, the worker determines what she thinks the unmet needs of the community are.
Which of the key issues in identifying unmet needs has the worker neglected to address?
    A. The different points of view regarding the issues, and whether there is any common ground
    B. Whether the stated problems and conversations with community residents reflect the same concerns
    C. How community residents define the issues
    D. What the residents talk about with one another in a community

24.____

25. Which of the following political styles should be used to promote an issue that could become controversial if it is perceived to involve major reforms?
    A. High-conflict, polarized
    B. High-conflict, consensual
    C. Moderate conflict, compromise-oriented
    D. Low-conflict, technical

25.____

KEY (CORRECT ANSWERS)

1.	C	11.	D
2.	A	12.	B
3.	B	13.	A
4.	B	14.	B
5.	B	15.	A
6.	D	16.	A
7.	A	17.	D
8.	B	18.	B
9.	D	19.	C
10.	B	20.	B

21.	D
22.	A
23.	A
24.	A
25.	D

EXAMINATION SECTION

TEST 1

DIRECTIONS: Each question or incomplete statement is followed by several suggested answers or completions. Select the one that BEST answers the question or completes the statement. *PRINT THE LETTER OF THE CORRECT ANSWER IN THE SPACE AT THE RIGHT.*

1. A supervisor was given a booklet that showed a new work method that could save time. He didn't tell his men because he thought that they would get the booklet anyway.
   For the supervisor to have acted like this is a
   A. *good* idea, because he saves time and both of talking to the men
   B. *bad* idea, because he should make sure his men know about better work methods
   C. *good* idea, because the men would rather read about it themselves
   D. *bad* idea, because a supervisor should always show his men every memo he gets from higher authority

   1.____

2. A supervisor found it necessary to discipline two subordinates. One man had been operating his equipment in a wrong way, while the other man came to work late for three days in a row. The supervisor decided to talk to both men together.
   For the supervisor to deal with the problems in this way is a
   A. *good* idea because each man will learn about the difficulties of the other person and how to solve such difficulties
   B. *bad* idea because the supervisor should wait until he can bring a larger group together and save time in discussing such questions
   C. *good* idea because he will be able to get the men to see that their problems are related
   D. *bad* idea because he should meet with each man separately and give him his full attention

   2.____

3. A supervisor should try to make his men feel their jobs are important in order to
   A. get the men to say good things about their supervisor to his own superior
   B. get the men to think in terms of advancing to better jobs
   C. let higher management in the agency know that the supervisor is efficient
   D. help the men to be able to work more efficiently and enthusiastically

   3.____

4. A supervisor should know approximately how long it takes to do a particular kind of job CHIEFLY because he
   A. will know how much time to take if he has to do it himself
   B. will be able to tell his men to do it even faster
   C. can judge the performance of the person doing the job
   D. can retrain experienced employees in better work habits

   4.____

5. Supervisors often get their employees' opinions about better work methods because
   A. the men will know that they are respected
   B. the men would otherwise lose all their confidence in the supervisor
   C. the supervisor might find in this way a good suggestion he could use
   D. this is the best method for improvement of work methods

6. Right after you have trained your subordinates in doing a new job, you find that they seem to be doing all right, but that it will take them several days to finish. You also have several groups of men working at other locations.
   The MOST efficient way for you to make sure that the men continue doing the new job properly is to
   A. stay on that job with the men until it is finished just in case trouble develops
   B. visit the men every half hour until the job is done
   C. stay away from their job that day and visit the men the next day to ask them if they had any problems
   D. visit the men a few times each day until they finish the new job

7. Assume that one of your new employees is older than you are. You also think that he may be hard to get along with because he is older than you.
   The BEST way for you to avoid any problems with the older worker is for you to
   A. lay down the law immediately and tell the man he better not cause you any trouble
   B. treat the man just the way you would any other worker
   C. always ask the older worker for advice in the presence of all the men
   D. ignore the man entirely until he realizes that you are the boss

8. Assume that you have tried a new method suggested by one of your employees and find that it is easier and cheaper than the method you had been using.
   The PROPER thing for you to do NEXT is to
   A. say nothing to anyone but train your men to use the new method
   B. train your men to use the new method and tell your crew that you got the idea from one of the men
   C. continue using the old method because a supervisor should not use suggestions of his men
   D. have your crew learn the new method and take credit for the idea since you are the boss

9. Suppose you are a supervisor and your superior tells you that the way your men are doing a certain procedure is wrong and that you should re-train our men as soon as possible.
   When you begin to re-train the men, the FIRST thing you should do is to
   A. tell your men that a wrong procedure had been used and that a new method must be learned as a result
   B. train your employees in the new method with no explanation since you are the boss

C. tell the crew that your superior has just decided that everyone should learn a new method
D. tell the crew that your superior says your method is wrong but that you don't agree with this

10. It is BAD practice to criticize a man in front of the other men because
    A. people will think you are too strict
    B. it is annoying to anyone who walks by
    C. it is embarrassing to the man concerned
    D. it will antagonize the other men

11. A supervisor decides not to put his two best men on a work detail because he knows that they won't like it.
    For the supervisor to make the work assignment this way is a
    A. *good* idea because it is only fair to give your best men a break once in a while
    B. *bad* idea because you should treat all of your me fairly and not show favoritism
    C. *good* idea because you save the strength of these men for another job
    D. *bad* idea because more of the men should be exempted from the assignment

12. Suppose you are a supervisor and you find it inconvenient to obey an established procedure set by your agency. You think another procedure would be better.
    The BEST thing to do first about this procedure that you don't like is for you to
    A. obey the procedure even if you don't to and suggest your idea to your own supervisor
    B. disregard the procedure because a supervisor is supposed to have some privileges
    C. follow the procedure some of the time but ignore it when the men are not watching
    D. organize a group of other supervisors to get the procedure changed

13. A supervisor estimated that it would take his crew one workday per week to do a certain job each week. However, after a month he noticed that the job averaged two and a half days a week and this delayed other jobs that had to be done.
    The FIRST thing that the supervisor should do in this case is to
    A. call him men together and warn them that they will get a poor work evaluation if they do not work harder
    B. talk to each man personally, asking him to work harder on the job
    C. go back and study the maintenance job by himself to see if more men should be assigned to the job
    D. write his boss a report describing in detail how much time it is taking the men to do the job

14. An employee complains to you that some of the work assignments are too difficult to do alone.
Which of the following is the BEST way for you to handle this complaint?
    A. Go with him to see exactly what he does and why he finds it so difficult
    B. Politely tell the man that he has to do the job or be brought up on charges
    C. Tell the man to send his complaint to the head of your agency
    D. Sympathize with the man and give him easier jobs

15. The BEST way for a supervisor to keep control of his work assignments is to
    A. ask the men to report to him immediately when their jobs are finished
    B. walk around the buildings once a week and get a first-hand view of what is being done
    C. keep his ears open for problems and complaints, but leave the men aloe to do the work
    D. write up a work schedule and check it periodically against the actual work done

16. A supervisor made a work schedule for his men. At the bottom of it, he wrote, *No changes or exceptions will be made in this schedule for any reason.*
For the supervisor to have made this statement is
    A. *good*, because the men will respect the supervisor for his attitude
    B. *bad*, because there are emergencies and special situations that occur
    C. *good*, because each man will know exactly what is expected of him
    D. *bad*, because the men should expect that no changes will ever be made in the work schedule without written permission

17. Which one of the following would NOT be a result of a well-planned work schedule?
The schedule
    A. makes efficient use of the time of the staff
    B. acts as a checklist for an important job that might be left out
    C. will give an idea of the work to a substitute supervisor
    D. shows at a glance who the best men are

18. A new piece of equipment you have ordered is delivered. You are familiar with it, but the men under you who will use it do not know the equipment.
Of the following methods, which is the BEST to take in explaining to them how to operate this equipment?
    A. Ask the men to watch other crews using the equipment
    B. Show one reliable man how to operate the equipment and ask him to teach the other men
    C. Ask the men to read the instructions in the manual for the equipment
    D. Call the men together and show them how to operate the equipment

19. One supervisor assigns work to his men by calling his crew together each week and describing what has to be done that week. He then tells them to arrange individual assignments among themselves and to work as a team during the week.

This method of scheduling work is a
- A. *good* idea because this guarantees that the men will work together
- B. *bad* idea because responsibility for doing the job is poorly fixed
- C. *good* idea because the men will finish the job in less time, working together
- D. *bad* idea because the supervisor should always stay with his men

20. Suppose that an employee came to his supervisor with a problem concerning his assignment.
    For the supervisor to listen to his problem is a
    - A. *good* idea because a supervisor should always take time off to talk when one of his men wants to talk
    - B. *bad* idea because the supervisor should not be bothered during the work day
    - C. *good* idea because it is the job of the supervisor to deal with problems of job assignment
    - D. *bad* idea because the employee could start annoying the supervisor with all sorts of problems

21. Suppose that on the previous afternoon you were looking for an experienced employee in order to give him an emergency job and he was missing from his job location. The next morning, he tells you that he got sick suddenly and had to go home, but could not tell you since you were not around. He has never done this before.
    What should you do?
    - A. Tell the man he is excused and that in such circumstances he did the wisest thing
    - B. Bring the man up on charges because whatever he says he could still have notified you
    - C. Have the man examined by a doctor to see if he really was sick the day before
    - D. Explain to the mean that he should make every effort to tell you or to get a message to you if he must leave

22. An employee had a grievance and went to his supervisor about it. The employee was not satisfied with the way the supervisor tried to help him and told him so. Yet, the supervisor had done everything he could under the circumstances.
    The PROPER action for the supervisor to take at this time is to
    - A. politely tell the employee that there is nothing more for the supervisor to do about the problem
    - B. let the employee know how he can bring his complaint to a higher authority
    - C. tell the employee that he must solve the problem on his own since he did not want to follow the supervisor's advice
    - D. suggest to the employee that he ask for another supervisor for assistance

23. In which of the following situations is it BEST to give your men spoken rather than written orders?
    A. You want your men to have a record of the instructions.
    B. Spoken instructions are less likely to be forgotten.
    C. An emergency situation has arisen in which there is no time to write up instructions.
    D. There are instructions on time and leave regulations which are complicated.

23._____

24. One of your employees tells you that a week ago he had a small accident on the job but he did not bother telling you because he was able to continue working.
    For the employee not to have told his supervisor about the accident was
    A. *good*, because the accident was a small one
    B. *bad*, because all accidents should be reported, no matter how small
    C. *good*, because the supervisor should be bothered only for important matters
    D. *bad*, because having an accident is one way to get excused for the day

24._____

25. For a supervisor to deal with each of his subordinate in exactly the same manner is
    A. *poor*, because each man presents a different problem and there is no one way of handling all problems
    B. *good*, because once a problem is handled with one man, he can handle another man with the same problem
    C. *poor*, because the men will resent it if they are not handled each in a better way than others
    D. *good*, because this assures fair and impartial treatment of each subordinate

25._____

KEY (CORRECT ANSWERS)

1. B
2. D
3. D
4. C
5. C

6. D
7. B
8. B
9. A
10. C

11. B
12. A
13. C
14. A
15. D

16. B
17. D
18. D
19. B
20. C

21. D
22. B
23. C
24. B
25. A

TEST 2

DIRECTIONS: Each question or incomplete statement is followed by several suggested answers or completions. Select the one that BEST answers the question or completes the statement. *PRINT THE LETTER OF THE CORRECT ANSWER IN THE SPACE AT THE RIGHT.*

1. Jim Johnson has been on your staff for over four years. He has always been a conscientious and productive worker. About a month ago, his wife died; and since that time, his work performance has been very poor.
   As his supervisor, which one of the following is the BEST way for you to deal with this situation?
   A. Allow Jim as much time as he needs to overcome his grief and hope that his work performance improves
   B. Meet with Jim to discuss ways to improve his performance
   C. Tell Jim directly that you are more concerned with his work performance than with his personal problem
   D. Prepare disciplinary action on Jim as soon as possible

   1.____

2. You are responsible for the overall operation of a storehouse which is divided into two sections. Each section has its own supervisor. You have decided to make several complex changes in the storekeeping procedures which will affect both sections.
   Of the following, the BEST way to make sure that these changes are understood by the two supervisors is for you to
   A. meet with both supervisors to discuss the changes
   B. issue a memorandum to each supervisor explaining the changes
   C. post the changes where the supervisors are sure to see them
   D. instruct one supervisor to explain the changes to the other supervisor

   2.____

3. You have called a meeting of all your subordinates to tell them what has to be done on a new project in which they will all be involved. Several times during the meeting, you ask if there are any questions about what you have told them.
   Of the following, to ask the subordinates whether there are any questions during the meeting can BEST be described as
   A. *inadvisable*, because it interferes with their learning about the new project
   B. *advisable*, because you will find out what they don't understand and have a chance to clear up any problems they may have
   C. *inadvisable*, because it makes the meeting too long and causes the subordinates to lose interest in the new project
   D. *advisable*, because it gives you a chance to learn which of your subordinates are paying attention to what you say

   3.____

4. As a supervisor, you are responsible for seeing to it that absenteeism does not become a problem among your subordinates.
   Which one of the following is NOT an acceptable way of controlling the problem of excessive absences?

   4.____

2 (#2)

    A. Distribute a written statement to your staff on the policies regarding absenteeism in your organization
    B. Arrange for workers who have the fewest absences to talk to those workers who have the most absences
    C. Let your subordinates know that a record is being kept of all absences
    D. Arrange for counseling of those employees who are frequently absent

5. One of your supervisors has been an excellent worker for the past two years. There are no promotion opportunities for this worker in the foreseeable future. Due to the city's present budget crisis, a salary increase is not possible.
Under the circumstances, which one of the following actions on your part would be MOST likely to continue to motivate this worker?
    A. Tell the worker that times are bad all over and jobs are hard to find
    B. Give the worker less work and easier assignments
    C. Tell the worker to try to look for a better paying job elsewhere
    D. Seek the worker's advice often and show that the suggestions provided are appreciated

5._____

6. As a supervisor in a warehouse, it is important that you use your available work force to its fullest potential.
Which one of the following actions on your part is MOST likely to increase the effectiveness of your work force?
    A. Assigning more workers to a job than the number actually needed
    B. Eliminating all job training to allow more time for work output
    C. Using your best workers on jobs that average workers can do
    D. Making sure that all materials and equipment used are maintained in good working order

6._____

7. You learn that your storage area will soon be undergoing changes which will affect the work of your subordinates. You decide not to tell your subordinates about what is to happen.
Of the following, your action can BEST be described as
    A. *wise*, because your subordinates will learn of the changes for themselves
    B. *unwise*, because your subordinates should be advised about what is to happen
    C. *wise*, because it is better for your subordinates to continue working without being disturbed by such news
    D. *unwise*, because the work of your subordinates will gradually slow down

7._____

8. In making plans for the operation of your unit, you are MOST likely to see these plans carried out successfully if you
    A. allow your staff to participate in developing these plans
    B. do not spend any time on the minor details of these plans
    C. base these plans on the past experiences of others
    D. allow these plans to interact with outside activities in other units

8._____

9. As a supervisor in charge of the total operation of a food supply warehouse, you find vandalism to be a potentially serious problem. On occasion, trespassers have gained entrance into the facility by climbing over an unprotected 8-foot fence surrounding the warehouse whose dimensions measure 100 feet by 100 feet.
Assuming that all of the following would be equally effective ways in preventing these breaches in security in the situation described above, which one would be LEAST costly?
    A. Using two trained guard dogs to roam freely throughout the facility at night
    B. Hiring a security guard to patrol the facility after working hours
    C. Installing tape razor wire on top of the fence surrounding the facility
    D. Installing an electronic burglar alarm system requiring the installation of a new fence

10. The area for which you have program responsibility has undergone recent changes. Your staff is now required to perform many new tasks, and morale is low.
The LEAST effective way for you to improve long-term staff morale would be to
    A. develop support groups to discuss problems
    B. involve staff in job development
    C. maintain a comfortable social environment within the group
    D. adequately plan and give assignments in a timely manner

11. As a supervisor in a large office, one of your subordinate supervisors stops you in the middle of the office and complains loudly that he is being treated unfairly. The rest of the staff ceases work and listens to the complaint.
The MOST appropriate action for you to take in this situation is to
    A. ignore this unprofessional behavior and continue on your way
    B. tell the supervisor that his behavior is unprofessional and he should learn how to conduct himself
    C. explain to the supervisor why you believe he is not being treated unfairly
    D. ask the supervisor to come to your office at a specific time to discuss the matter

12. You are told that one of your subordinates is distributing literature which attempts to recruit individuals to join a particular organization. Several workers complain that their rights are being violated.
Of the following, the BEST action for you to take FIRST is to
    A. ignore the situation because no harm is being done
    B. discuss the matter further with your supervisor
    C. ask the worker to stop distributing the literature
    D. tell the workers that they do not have to read the material

13. You have been assigned to develop a short training course for a recently issued procedure.
In designing this course, which of the following statements is the LEAST important for you to consider?

A. The learning experience must be interesting and meaningful in terms of the staff member's job.
B. The method of teaching must be strictly followed in order to develop successful learning experiences.
C. The course content should incorporate the rules and regulations of the agency.
D. The procedure should be consistent with the agency's objectives.

14. As a supervisor, there are several newly-promoted employees under your supervision. Each of these employees is subject to a probationary period PRIMARILY to
    A. assess the employee's performance to see if the employee should be retained or removed from the position
    B. give the employee the option to return to his former employment if the employee is unhappy in the new position
    C. give the employee an opportunity to learn the duties and responsibilities of the position
    D. judge the employee's potential for upward mobility in the future

14._____

15. An employee under your supervision rushes into your office to tell you he has just received a telephone bomb threat.
    As the administrative supervisor, the FIRST thing you should do is
    A. evacuate staff from the floor
    B. call the police and building security
    C. advise your administrator
    D. do a preliminary search

15._____

16. After reviewing the Absence Control form for a unit under your supervision, you find that one of your staff members has a fifth undocumented sick leave within a six-month period.
    In this situation, the FIRST action you should take is to
    A. discuss the seriousness of the matter with the staff member when he returns to work and fully document the details of the discussion
    B. review the case with the location director and warn the staff member that future use of sick leave will be punished
    C. submit the proper disciplinary forms to ensure that the staff member is penalized for excessive absences
    D. request that the timekeeper put the staff member on doctor's note restriction

16._____

17. A subordinate supervisor recently assigned to your office begins his first conference with you by saying that he has learned something that another supervisor is doing that you should know about.
    After hearing this statement, of the following, the BEST approach for you to take is to
    A. explain to the supervisor that the conference is to discuss his work and not that of his co-workers
    B. tell the supervisor that you do not encourage a spy system among the staff you supervise

17._____

C. tell the supervisor that you will listen to his report only if the other supervisor is present
D. allow the supervisor to continue talking until you have enough information to make a decision on how best to respond

18. Assume that you are a supervisor recently assigned to a new unit. You notice that, for the past few days, one of the employees in your unit whose work is about average has been stopping work at about four o'clock and has been spending the rest of the afternoon relaxing at his desk.
The BEST of the following actions for you to take in this situation is to
    A. assign more work to this employee since it is apparent that he does not have enough work to keep him busy
    B. observe the employee's conduct more closely for about ten days before taking any more positive action
    C. discuss the matter with the employee, pointing out to him how he can use the extra hour daily to raise the level of his job performance
    D. question the previous supervisor in charge of the unit in order to determine whether he had sanctioned such conduct when he supervised that unit

18.____

19. A new supervisor was assigned to your program four months ago. Although he tries hard, he has been unable to meet certain standards because he still has a lot to learn. As his supervisor, you are required to submit performance evaluations within a few days.
How would you rate this employee on the tasks where he fails to meet standards because of lack of experience?
    A. Satisfactory   B. Conditional
    C. Unsatisfactory   D. Unratable

19.____

20. You find that there is an important procedural error in a memo which you distributed to your staff several days ago.
The BEST approach for you to take at this time is to
    A. send a corrected memo to the staff, indicating what prior error was made
    B. send a corrected memo to the staff without mentioning the prior error
    C. tell the staff about the error at the next monthly staff meeting
    D. place the corrected memo on the office bulletin board

20.____

21. Your superior asks you, a supervisor, about the status of the response to a letter from a public official concerning a client's case. When you ask the subordinate who was assigned to prepare the response to give you the letter, the subordinate denies that it was given to him. You are certain that the subordinate has the letter, but is withholding it because the response has not yet been prepared.
Of the following, in order to secure the letter from the subordinate, you should FIRST
    A. accuse the subordinate of lying and demand that the letter be given to you immediately
    B. say that you would consider it a personal favor if the subordinate would find the letter

21.____

C. continue to question the subordinate until he admits to having been given the letter
D. offer a face-saving solution, such as asking the subordinate to look again for the letter

22. As a supervisor, you have been assigned to write a few paragraphs to be included in the agency's annual report, describing a public service agency department this year as compared to last year.
Which of the following elements basic to the agency is LEAST likely to have changed since last year?
A. Mission B. Structure C. Technology D. Personnel

23. As a supervisor, you have been informed that a grievance has been filed against you, accusing you of assigning a subordinate to out-of-title tasks.
Of the following, the BEST approach for you to take is to
A. waive the grievance so that it will proceed to a Step II hearing
B. immediately change the subordinate's assignment to avoid future problems
C. respond to the grievance, giving appropriate reasons for the assignment
D. review the job description to ensure that the subordinate's tasks are not out-of-title

24. Which of the following is NOT a correct statement about agency group training programs in a public service agency?
A. Training sessions continue for an indefinite period of time.
B. Group training sessions are planned for designated personnel.
C. Training groups are organized formally through administrative planning.
D. Group training is task-centered and aimed toward accomplishing specific educational goals.

25. As a supervisor, you have submitted a memo to your superior requesting a conference to discuss the performance of a manager under your supervision. The memo states that the manager has a good working relationship with her staff; however, she tends to interpret agency policy too liberally and shows poor administrative skills by missing some deadlines and not keeping proper controls.
Which of the following steps should NOT be taken in order to prepare for this conference with your superior?
A. Collect and review all your notes regarding the manager's prior performance.
B. Outline your agenda so that you will have sufficient time to discuss the situation.
C. Tell the manager that you will be discussing her performance with your superior.
D. Clearly define objectives which will focus on improving the manager's performance.

KEY (CORRECT ANSWERS)

1.	B		11.	D
2.	A		12.	C
3.	B		13.	B
4.	B		14.	A
5.	D		15.	B
6.	D		16.	A
7.	B		17.	D
8.	A		18.	C
9.	C		19.	B
10.	C		20.	A

21. D
22. A
23. C
24. A
25. C

EXAMINATION SECTION

TEST 1

DIRECTIONS: Each question or incomplete statement is followed by several suggested answers or completions. Select the one that BEST answers the question or completes the statement. *PRINT THE LETTER OF THE CORRECT ANSWER IN THE SPACE AT THE RIGHT.*

1. Assume that a supervisor finds that his employees have become fatigued from doing a very long and repetitious job.
   The one of the following which would be the BEST way to relieve this fatigue is to
   A. assign other work so that the employees can switch to different assignments in the middle of the day
   B. let the employees listen to a radio while they work
   C. break the job down into very small parts so that each employee can concentrate on one simple task
   D. allow the employees to take frequent rest periods

1.____

2. Assume that one of your subordinates is injured and will be out for at least six weeks.
   Of the following, the BEST way to handle the work normally assigned to this person is to
   A. allow the work to remain uncompleted until the injured person returns, since he is the one who can BEST do this work
   B. divide this work equally among the persons under your supervision who can do this work
   C. do all the work yourself
   D. give the injured person's work to the most efficient member of your staff

2.____

3. Suppose that another supervisor tells you about a new way to organize some of your unit's work. The idea sounds good to you. However, before you were in this unit, a similar plan was tried and it failed.
   The MOST important thing for you to do FIRST is to
   A. find out why the previous attempt failed
   B. suggest that the other supervisor tell his idea to top management
   C. try the plan to see whether it works
   D. find proof that the plan has worked elsewhere

3.____

4. One of your subordinates comes to you with a grievance. You discuss it with him so that you may fully understand the problem as he sees it.
   However, since you are uncertain as to the proper answer, you should
   A. tell him that you cannot help him with this problem
   B. tell him that you will have to check further and make an appointment to see him again
   C. send him to see your immediate superior for a solution to the problem
   D. ask him to find out from his co-workers whether this problem has come up before

4.____

5. A supervisor reprimanded one of his subordinates severely for making a serious error in judgment while performing an assignment for which he had volunteered.
The supervisor's action was
   A. *incorrect*, chiefly because in the future the worker will probably try to avoid taking on responsibility
   B. *correct*, chiefly because this will insure that the worker will not make the same mistake in the future
   C. *correct*, chiefly because the worker should be discouraged from using his own judgment on the job
   D. *incorrect*, chiefly because the reprimand came too late to correct the error that had already been made

6. Of the following, the BEST way for a supervisor to inform all his subordinates of a change in lunch rules is, in MOST cases, to
   A. call a staff meeting
   B. tell each one individually
   C. issue a memorandum
   D. tell one or two employees to pass the word around

7. For a supervisor to assign work giving only general instructions to his subordinate would be advisable when
   A. the supervisor is confident that the worker knows how to do the job
   B. the assignment is a simple one
   C. the subordinate is himself a supervisory employee
   D. errors in the work will not cause serious delay

8. One of the DISADVANTAGES of setting minimum standards of performance for custodial employees is that
   A. such standards eliminate the basis for evaluating employees
   B. the custodial employees may keep their performance at the minimum level
   C. standards are always subject to change
   D. the supervisor may feel that his initiative is being restricted

9. One of your subordinates has been functioning below his usual level. You feel that something of a personal nature may be affecting his work. When you ask him casually whether anything is wrong, he says everything is fine.
As a next step, it would be BEST to
   A. make frequent casual and humorous comments about the poor quality of his work but refrain, at this time, from any serious discussion
   B. warn him that failure to maintain his customary level of performance might result in disciplinary action
   C. express your concern privately and reveal your interest in the reason for his change in work performance
   D. discuss with him the work of another employee, suggesting that the other employee would be a good example to follow

10. Assume you are teaching a new job to one of your subordinates. After you have demonstrated the job, you can BEST maintain the worker's interest by
    A. showing him training films about the job
    B. giving him printed material that explains why the job is important
    C. having him observe other workers do the job
    D. letting him attempt to do the job by himself under supervision

11. *Insubordination is sometimes a protest against inferior or arbitrary leadership.*
    For the supervisor, the MOST basic implication of the above statement is:
    A. Accusations of insubordination are easy to make, but usually difficult to prove.
    B. Insubordination cannot be permitted if an organization wishes to remain effective.
    C. When an employee discusses an order instead of carrying it out, he has not understood it.
    D. When an employee questions an order, review it to make sure it is reasonable.

12. In appraising a subordinate's mistakes, a supervisor should ALWAYS consider the
    A. absolute number of mistakes, without regard to severity
    B. number of mistakes in proportion to the number of decisions made
    C. total number of mistakes made by other, regardless of assignment
    D. number of mistakes which were discovered upon higher review

13. If you are the supervisor of an office in which the work frequently involves lifting heavy boxes, you should instruct your staff in the proper method of lifting to avoid injury.
    In giving these instructions, you should stress that a person lifting heavy objects MUST
    A. keep his feet close together
    B. bend at the waist
    C. keep his back as straight as possible
    D. use his back muscles to straighten up

14. Of the following, the BEST qualified supervisor is one who
    A. knows the basic principles and procedures of all the jobs which he supervises
    B. has detailed working knowledge of all aspects of the job he supervises but knows little about principles of supervision
    C. is able to do exceptionally well at least one of the jobs which he supervises and as some knowledge of the others
    D. knows little or nothing about most of the jobs which he supervises but knows the principles of supervision

15. The rate at which an employee will learn will vary according to a number of considerations.
Of the following, which is LEAST likely to be controllable by the supervisor or the trainer? The
    A. manner in which the material is presented
    B. state of readiness of the learner
    C. scheduling of practice sessions
    D. nature of the material

16. When considering whether to use written material rather than oral instructions as a means of giving instructions to employees, the one of the following which should be given GREATEST consideration is the employees'
    A. personal preferences   B. attitude toward supervision
    C. general educational level   D. salary level

17. Assume that one of your subordinates has been assigned to attend job training classes.
The one of the following which would probably be the BEST evidence of the success of the course is that the employee
    A. feels that he has learned something
    B. continues to study after the course is over
    C. has had a good class record
    D. improves in his work performance

18. Of the following, the situation LEAST likely to result if a supervisor shows favoritism toward particular employees is
    A. laxity in the work of the favored employees
    B. resentment from the other, less-favored employees
    C. increased ability among the favored employees
    D. lowering of morale among employees

19. The one of the following reasons for evaluating employees' performance, whether done formally or informally, which is NOT considered to be POSITIVE in nature is to
    A. give individual counsel to employees
    B. motivate employees toward improvement
    C. provide recognition of superior service
    D. set penalties for substandard performance

20. Assume that, because there has been an unexpected and temporary increase in the short-term work of your unit, you have had temporarily assigned to you several staff members from another agency.
Of the following, in dealing with these employees, it would be LEAST advisable to
    A. assign them to long-term projects
    B. organize tasks so that they can begin work immediately
    C. set standards, making allowances to give them time to learn your ways
    D. direct them in the same way, in general, as you do your regular staff

21. It has been suggested that one way to increase employee productivity would be to require employees dealing with the public to have proficiency in a relevant foreign language.
Of the following, the MAJOR reason for implementing such a proposal, from the viewpoint of effective public administration, would be to
    A. encourage the foreign-born to learn English
    B. exchange information more rapidly and accurately
    C. increase the public prestige of the agency
    D. stimulate ethnic pride among all groups

21.____

22. Assume that the clerk who normally keeps your unit's records will be on vacation for four weeks.
If other clerks are equally qualified to keep these records, your BEST choice to replace the clerk would be the person who
    A. has skills which are needed least for other duties during this period
    B. volunteers for this work
    C. is next in turn for a special assignment
    D. has handled this task before

22.____

23. Assume that you have under your supervision several young clerical employees who have the bad habit of fooling around when they should be working.
Of the following, the BEST disciplinary action to take would be to
    A. ignore it; these young people will outgrow it
    B. join in the fun briefly in order to bring it to a quicker end each time it occurs
    C. bring to their attention the fact that this behavior is not acceptable and if it continues shift the make-up of the group to keep these young persons apart
    D. warn them that this type of behavior is reason for dismissal and be quick to make an example of the first one who starts it again

23.____

24. Seeking the advice of community leaders has human relations value for a public agency in planning or executing its programs CHIEFLY because it
    A. allows for the keeping of careful records concerning individual suggestions
    B. lets community leaders know that the agency has regard for their opinions
    C. permits the agency to state in writing which programs seem most appropriate
    D. unifies community leaders against the programs of competing private agencies

24.____

25. Good community relations is often action-oriented.
Which of the following activities of a public agency is LEAST likely to be considered as action-oriented by the people of a local community?
    A. Conducting a survey to gather information about the local community
    B. Extending the use of a facility to those previously excluded
    C. Providing a service that was formerly non-existent
    D. Removing something considered objectionable by the local community

25.____

KEY (CORRECT ANSWERS)

1.	A		11.	D
2.	B		12.	B
3.	A		13.	C
4.	B		14.	A
5.	A		15.	B
6.	C		16.	C
7.	A		17.	D
8.	B		18.	D
9.	C		19.	D
10.	D		20.	A

21. B
22. A
23. C
24. B
25. A

TEST 2

DIRECTIONS: Each question or incomplete statement is followed by several suggested answers or completions. Select the one that BEST answers the question or completes the statement. *PRINT THE LETTER OF THE CORRECT ANSWER IN THE SPACE AT THE RIGHT.*

1. Methods of communication with employees are of three types: oral, written, and visual.
A MAJOR advantage of the written word is that it
    A. insures that content will remain unchanged no matter how many persons may be involved in its transmission
    B. facilitates two-way communication in delicate or confidential situations
    C. strengthens chain-of-command procedures in transmission of information and instruction by requiring the use of prescribed channels
    D. encourages the active participation of employees in the solution of complicated problems

1.____

2. The use of the conference technique in training often requires more preparatory work on the part of the trainer than does a good lecture PRIMARILY because
    A. a conference would cover material of a more technical nature
    B. the trainer will be required to supply more printed material to the participants
    C. a conference usually involves a greater number of trainees
    D. the trainer must be prepared for a wide variety of possible occurrences

2.____

3. The one of the following which is NOT an advantage of the lecture over most other methods of training is that it can be given
    A. over the radio or on record   B. to large numbers of trainees
    C. without interruptions   D. with little preparation

3.____

4. Of the following, the one which is LEAST appropriate as a purpose for using an employee attitude survey is to
    A. develop a supervisory training program
    B. learn the identity of dissatisfied employees
    C. re-evaluate employee relations policies
    D. re-orient publications designed for employees

4.____

5. The competent trainer seeks to become knowledgeable both in the work of the agency and in the duties of the positions for which he is to conduct training. Of the following, the GREATEST practical value that result when the trainer gains such knowledge is that
    A. he will be more likely to instruct employees to perform their work in a manner consistent with actual practice
    B. all levels of staff will be favorably impressed by a display of interest in the agency and its work
    C. employees will become familiar with the trainer and will not consider him an outsider
    D. the trainer will gain an accurate picture of the capacity of each employee for training

5.____

6. Assume that you, the supervisor of a small office, are involved in planning the reorganization of your bureau's work. Management has decided not to inform your staff of the reorganization until the plans are completed.
If one of your subordinates tells you that he has heard a rumor about reorganization of the department, you should reply that
   A. the reorganization involves the bureau, not the department
   B. you haven't heard anything about departmental reorganization and that he should stop spreading rumors
   C. you will inform your staff at the appropriate time if any definite plans are made involving a reorganization
   D. you do not know what is being planned but will ask your superior for details

7. Of the following training methods, the one in which the trainee's role is usually LEAST active is the _____ method.
   A. case-study   B. conference
   C. group discussion   D. lecture

8. Differences in morale between two work groups can sometimes be attributed to differences in the supervision they receive.
Of the following, the behavior MOST characteristic of a supervisor of a group with high morale is that he
   A. assigns the least difficult tasks to employees with the most seniority
   B. is concerned primarily with his ultimate responsibility, production
   C. delegates authority and responsibility to his staff
   D. is lenient with his workers when they violate rules

9. Informal performance evaluations of individual employees, prepared systematically and regularly over a period of several years, are considered to be useful to a supervisor PRIMARILY because
   A. he will be able to assign tasks based only on these records
   B. unlike formal records, since they are fitted to the characteristics of individual employees, they provide for quick comparisons
   C. he need not discuss them with employees, since they are informal
   D. whatever personnel action he recommends can be substantiated by cumulative records

10. When instructing first-line supervisors in the proper method of evaluating the performance of probationary employees, it is LEAST important for a higher-level supervisor to
    A. explain in detail the standards to be used
    B. inform them of the possibility of higher management review
    C. caution them concerning common errors of evaluation
    D. mention the purposes of probationary employee evaluation

11. Assume that your agency is considering abolishing its official performance rating system but that you, a supervisor of a fairly large office, would like to devise a system for your own use.
    The FIRST step in setting up a system would be to
    A. decide what factors and personal characteristics are important and should be rated
    B. compare several rating methods to see which would be easiest to use
    C. have a private conference with each employee to discuss his performance
    D. set specific standards of employee performance, allowing your workers to make suggestions

12. The basic organizational structure of a municipal agency may have come about for several reasons.
    Of the following, the MOST important influence on the nature of its structure is the agency's
    A. professional attitude   B. public reputation
    C. overall goal   D. staff morale

13. The term *formal organization* refers to that organization structure agreed upon by top management whereas the term *informal organization* refers to the more spontaneous and flexible organizational ties developed by subordinates.
    The one of the following which BEST describes the usual *informal organization* is that it represents a(n)
    A. destructive system of relationships which should be eliminated
    B. concealed system of relationships whose goals are the same as management's
    C. actual system of relationships which should be recognized
    D. dysfunctional system of relationships which should be ignored

14. The reluctance of supervisors to delegate work to subordinates when they should is GENERALLY due to the supervisor's
    A. feelings of insecurity in work situations
    B. need to acquire additional experience
    C. inability to exercise control over his subordinates
    D. lack of technical knowledge

15. Assume that you have just been made the supervisor of a group of people you did not know before.
    For you to talk casually with each of your new subordinates with the purpose of getting to know them personally would be
    A. *advisable*, chiefly because subordinates have more confidence in a supervisor who shows personal interest in them
    B. *inadvisable*, chiefly because subordinates resent having their supervisor ask about their outside interests
    C. *advisable*, chiefly because one of the supervisor's main concerns should be to help his subordinates with their personal problems
    D. *inadvisable*, chiefly because a supervisor should not allow his relations with his subordinates to be influenced by their personalities

16. It has been found that high-producing subdivisions of organizations usually have supervisors whose behavior is employee-centered, whereas low-producing units usually have supervisors whose behavior is work-centered.
Therefore, it could be concluded from these findings that
    A. a high-producing unit may cause a supervisor to be authoritarian
    B. a low-producing unit may cause a supervisor to be work-centered
    C. close supervision usually increases production
    D. employee-centered leadership may reduce production

16.____

17. A recent study in managerial science showed that, as the amount of praise increased and amount of criticism decreased, the supervisor was more likely to be perceived by his subordinates as being
    A. concerned with their career advancement
    B. production oriented, through subtle intimidation
    C. seeking personal satisfaction, irrespective of production
    D. uncertain of the subordinates' reliability

17.____

18. The power to issue directives or instructions to employees is derived from employees as much as from management.
It follows MOST logically from this statement that
    A. attitudes toward management can be changed
    B. emphasis on discipline is needed
    C. authority is dependent upon acceptance
    D. employees should be properly supervised for work to be done

18.____

19. "In the decision-making process, it is a rare problem that has only one possible solution. Such a solution should be suspected of being nothing but a plausible argument for a preconceived idea."
The author of the foregoing quotation apparently does NOT believe that
    A. there is usually only one possible solution to a problem
    B. the risks involved in any solution should be weighed against expected gains
    C. each alternative should be evaluated to determine the effort needed
    D. actions should be based on the urgency of problems

19.____

20. The supervisor who relies on punitive discipline to enforce his authority is putting limits on the potential of his leadership. Fear of punishment may secure obedience, but it destroys initiative. Such a supervisor's autocratic methods have cut off upward communications.
Of the following, the major DISADVANTAGE of such autocratic behavior is that
    A. difficulties in the supervision of his subordinates will arise if limits are placed on the supervisor's responsibility
    B. policies that affect the public will be changed too frequently
    C. the supervisor will apply punishment subjectively rather than objectively
    D. instructions will be obeyed to the letter, regardless of changing circumstances

20.____

21. The need for a supervisor to carefully coordinate and direct the work of his unit increases as the work becomes 21.____
    A. more routine
    B. more specialized
    C. less complex
    D. less technical

22. The MAIN goal of discipline as used by a supervisor should be to 22.____
    A. keep the employees' respect
    B. influence behavior, so that work will be completed properly
    C. encourage the employees to work faster
    D. set an example for others

23. One of your subordinates has exhibited discourtesy and non-cooperation on several occasions. 23.____
    Of the following, the MOST appropriate attitude for you to adopt in dealing with this problem is that
    A. disciplinary measures for such an individual generally creates additional problems
    B. failure to correct such behavior may lead to worse offenses
    C. it is a mistake to make an issue out of minor infractions
    D. the harsher the medicine, the faster the cure

24. Assume that an employee has complained to you, his supervisor, that he cannot concentrate on his work because two of his co-workers make too much noise. You pay particular attention to these employees for several days and do not find them making excessive noise. 24.____
    The NEXT step you should take in handling this grievance is to
    A. have a talk with all three employees, urging them to cooperate and be considerate of one another
    B. arrange for the complainant to change his work location to a place away from the two co-workers
    C. talk to the complainant to find out if the complaint he made to you is the real cause of his dissatisfaction
    D. tell the complainant that you have found his grievance to be unfounded

25. In planning the application of an existing agency program to a local community, it is generally necessary to discover relevant problems and possibilities for service. 25.____
    Of the following, the BEST way to learn about such problems and possibilities for service would usually be to
    A. begin the program on a full-scale basis and await reactions
    B. seek opinions and advice from community residents and leaders
    C. hold staff meetings with agency employees who have worked in similar communities
    D. study official federal reports about already completed programs of the same kind

KEY (CORRECT ANSWERS)

1.	A	11.	A
2.	D	12.	C
3.	D	13.	C
4.	B	14.	A
5.	A	15.	A
6.	C	16.	B
7.	D	17.	A
8.	C	18.	C
9.	D	19.	A
10.	B	20.	D

21.	B
22.	B
23.	B
24.	C
25.	B

TEST 3

DIRECTIONS: Each question or incomplete statement is followed by several suggested answers or completions. Select the one that BEST answers the question or completes the statement. *PRINT THE LETTER OF THE CORRECT ANSWER IN THE SPACE AT THE RIGHT.*

1. Which of the following characteristics would be LEAST detrimental to a supervisor in his efforts to set up and maintain good relations with other supervisors with whom he must deal in the course of his duties?
   A. Not getting involved in consultation on any supervisory problems they might have
   B. Indicating that they should improve their supervising methods and offering suggestions on how to do so
   C. Emphasizing his own role as a member of management
   D. Sharing information which has proved useful in his unit

   1.____

2. Both trainers and supervisors might agree that there is usually a best way to do a particular job. Yet a supervisor or instructor sometimes does not teach a new employee the best way, the most efficient way, to do a complex job.
   Sometimes, in such cases, the supervisor temporarily changes the sequence of operations, increases the number of steps needed to do a job, or makes other changes in the method, which then deviates from the one considered most efficient.
   When is such a difference in approach MOST justified when teaching a new employee a complex job?
   A. When the changes in approach correspond to the learning ability of the new employee
   B. When the new employee's performance on the job is closely supervised to compensate for a change in approach
   C. Where the steps in performing the task have not been defined in a manual of procedures
   D. When the instructor has ideas of improving upon the methods for doing the job

   2.____

3. Considerable thought in the field of management is directed toward the advantages and disadvantages of authoritarian methods of influencing behavior, and, in the so-called authoritarian model, a nucleus of rather consistent ideas prevail.
   Which of the following is LEAST characteristic of an administrative system based on the authoritarian model?
   A. A conviction of a need for order and efficiency in a world consisting mainly of people who lack direction and incentive
   B. Rules and contracts are the basis for action, and decisions are made on an impersonal basis
   C. The right to give orders and instructions is inherent in the hierarchical arrangement of an organizational structure
   D. Realization that subordinates' needs for affiliation and recognition can contribute to management's objectives

   3.____

4. Of the following, the FIRST step in planning an operation is to 4.____
   A. obtain relevant information B. identify the goal to be achieved
   C. consider possible alternatives D. make necessary assignments

5. A supervisor who is extremely busy performing routine tasks is MOST likely 5.____
   making incorrect use of what basis principle of supervision?
   A. Homogeneous Assignment B. Span of Control
   C. Work Distribution D. Delegation of Authority

6. Controls help supervisors to obtain information from which they can determine 6.____
   whether their staffs are achieving planned goals.
   Which one of the following would be LEAST useful as a control device?
   A. Employee diaries B. Organization charts
   C. Periodic inspections D. Progress charts

7. A certain employee has difficulty in effectively performing a particular portion 7.____
   of his routine assignments, but his overall productivity is average.
   As a direct supervisor of this individual, your BEST course of action would be to
   A. attempt to develop the investigator's capacity to execute the
      problematical facets of his assignments
   B. diversify the investigator's work assignments in order to build up his
      confidence
   C. reassign the investigator to less difficult tasks
   D. request in a private conversation that the investigator improve his work
      output

8. A supervisor who uses persuasion as a means of supervising a unit would 8.____
   GENERALLY also use which of the following practices to supervise his unit?
   A. Supervises and control the staff with an authoritative attitude to indicate
      that he is a *take-charge* individual
   B. Make significant changes in the organizational operations so as to
      improve job efficiency
   C. Remove major communication barriers between himself, subordinates,
      and management
   D. Supervise everyday operations while being mindful of the problems of his
      subordinates

9. Whenever a supervisor in charge of a unit delegates a routine task to a capable 9.____
   subordinate, he tells him exactly how to do it.
   This practice is GENERALLY
   A. *desirable*, chiefly because good supervisors should be aware of the traits of their
      subordinates and delegate responsibilities to them accordingly
   B. *undesirable*, chiefly because only non-routine tasks should be delegated
   C. *desirable*, chiefly because a supervisor should frequently test the willingness of his
      subordinates to perform ordinary tasks
   D. *undesirable*, chiefly because a capable subordinate should usually be allowed to
      exercise his own discretion in doing a routine job

3 (#3)

10. The one of the following activities through which a supervisor BEST demonstrates leadership ability is by
    A. arranging periodic staff meetings in order to keep his subordinates informed about professional developments in the field of investigation
    B. frequently issuing definite orders and directives which will lessen the need for subordinates to make decisions in handling any investigations assigned to them
    C. devoting the major part of his time to supervising subordinates so as to stimulate continuous improvement
    D. setting aside time for self-development and research so as to improve the investigative techniques and procedures of his unit

10.____

11. The following three statements relate to supervision of employees:
    I. The assignment of difficult tasks that offer a challenge is more conducive to good morale than the assignment of easy tasks.
    II. The same general principles of supervision that apply to men are equally applicable to women.
    III. The best restraining program should cover all phases of an employee's work in a general manner.
    Which of the following choices lists ALL of the above statements that are generally CORRECT?
    A. II, III   B. I   C. I, II   D. I, II, III

11.____

12. Which of the following examples BEST illustrates the application of the *exception principle* as a supervisory technique? A(n)
    A. complex job is divided among several employees who work simultaneously to complete the whole job in a shorter time
    B. employee is required to complete any task delegated to him to such an extent that nothing is left for the superior who delegated the task except to approve it
    C. superior delegates responsibility to a subordinate but retains authority to make the final decisions
    D. superior delegates all work possible to his subordinates and retains that which requires his personal attention or performance

12.____

13. Assume that you are a supervisor. Your immediate superior frequently gives orders to your subordinates without your knowledge.
    Of the following, the MOST direct and effective way for you to handle this problem is to
    A. tell your subordinates to take orders only from you
    B. submit a report to higher authority in which you cite specific instances
    C. discuss it with your immediate superior
    D. find out to what extent you authority and prestige as a supervisor have been affected

13.____

14. In an agency which has as its primary purpose the protection of the public against fraudulent business practices, which of the following would GENERALLY be considered an auxiliary or staff rather than a line function?

14.____

A. Interviewing victims of frauds and advising them about their legal remedies
B. Daily activities directed toward prevention of fraudulent business practices
C. Keeping records and statistics about business violations reported and corrected
D. Follow-up inspections by investigators after corrective action has been taken

15. A supervisor can MOST effectively reduce the spread of false rumors through the *grapevine* by
    A. identifying and disciplining any subordinate responsible for initiating such rumors
    B. keeping his subordinates informed as much as possible about matters affecting them
    C. denying false rumors which might tend to lower staff morale and productivity
    D. making sure confidential matters are kept secure from access by unauthorized employees

16. A supervisor has tried to learn about the background, education, and family relationships of his subordinates through observation, personal contact, and inspection of their personnel records.
    These supervisory actions are GENERALLY
    A. *inadvisable*, chiefly because they may lead to charges of favoritism
    B. *advisable*, chiefly because they may make him more popular with his subordinates
    C. *inadvisable*, chiefly because his efforts may be regarded as an invasion of privacy
    D. *advisable*, chiefly because the information may enable him to develop better understanding of each of his subordinates

17. In an emergency situation, when action must be taken immediately, it is BEST for the supervisor to give orders in the form of
    A. direct commands, which are brief and precise
    B. requests, so that his subordinate will not become alarmed
    C. suggestions, which offer alternative courses of action
    D. implied directive, so that his subordinates may use their judgment in carrying them out

18. When demonstrating a new and complex procedure to a group of subordinates, it is ESSENTIAL that a supervisor
    A. go slowly and repeat the steps involved at least once
    B. show the employees common errors and the consequences of such errors
    C. go through the process at the usual speed so that the employees can see the rate at which they should work
    D. distribute summaries of the procedure during the demonstration and instruct his subordinates to refer to them afterwards

19. The PRIMARY value of office reports and procedures is to   19.____
    A. assist top management in controlling key agency functions
    B. measure job performance
    C. save time and labor
    D. control the activities and use of time of all staff members

20. Of the following, which is considered to be the GREATEST advantage of the   20.____
    oral report? It
    A. allows for accurate transmission of information from one individual to another
    B. presents an opportunity to discuss or clarify any immediate questions raised by the receiver of the report
    C. requires less office work to maintain records on actions taken when an oral report is involved
    D. takes only a short amount of time to plan and prepare material for an oral report

21. A supervisor who is to make a report about a job he has done can make an   21.____
    oral report of a written report.
    Of the following, which is the BEST time to make an oral report? When
    A. the work covers an emergency situation
    B. a record is needed for the files
    C. the report is channeled to other departments
    D. the report covers additional work he will do

22. Suppose that a new employee has been assigned to you. It is your   22.____
    responsibility to see to it that he understands how to fill out properly the forms
    he is required to use.
    What would be the BEST way to do this?
    A. Explain the use of each form to the new technician and show him how to fill them out
    B. Give the new employee a copy of each form he must use so that he can learn by studying them
    C. Ask an experienced worker to explain clearly to him how the forms should be filled out
    D. Tell the new employee that filling out forms is simple and he should follow the instructions on each form

23. As a supervisor, you want to have your staff take part in improving work   23.____
    methods.
    Of the following, the BEST way to do this is to
    A. make critical appraisals of their work frequently
    B. encourage them to make suggestions
    C. make no change without their approval
    D. hold regular staff meetings

24. A good relationship with other supervisors is important to a senior supervisor. Close cooperation among supervisory personnel is MOST likely to result in
    A. increasing the probability for support of supervisory actions and decisions
    B. stimulating supervisors to achieve higher status in the organization
    C. helping to control the flow of work within a unit
    D. a clearer definition of the responsibilities of individual supervisors

25. Which of the following is MOST likely to gain a supervisor the respect and cooperation of his staff?
    A. Assigning the most difficult jobs to the experienced staff members
    B. Giving each staff member the same number of assignments
    C. Assigning jobs according to each staff member's ability
    D. Giving each staff member the same types of assignments

KEY (CORRECT ANSWERS)

1.	D		11.	C
2.	A		12.	D
3.	D		13.	C
4.	B		14.	C
5.	D		15.	B
6.	B		16.	D
7.	A		17.	A
8.	D		18.	A
9.	D		19.	A
10.	C		20.	B

21.	A
22.	A
23.	B
24.	A
25.	C

EXAMINATION SECTION
TEST 1

DIRECTIONS: Each question or incomplete statement is followed by several suggested answers or completions. Select the one that BEST answers the question or completes the statement. *PRINT THE LETTER OF THE CORRECT ANSWER IN THE SPACE AT THE RIGHT.*

1. For a large public park and recreation department, it is generally agreed that the key to productivity is

    A. contracting and leasing arrangements
    B. the effective management of personnel
    C. cost-benefit analysis
    D. appealing to private foundations for funds

    1.____

2. In a park and recreation setting, four conditions must be present in a situation in order for the department to be found legally negligent, and therefore liable, in the case of an accident. Which of the following is NOT one of these conditions?

    A. Proof of injury or damage
    B. Legal responsibility for the participant
    C. The participant's lack of an employment relationship to the department
    D. The department's failure to take reasonable care

    2.____

3. In a park and recreation department, the MOST effective approach to problem-solving is generally described as

    A. group-centered
    B. authoritarian
    C. decisions by higher authorities
    D. an analysis by planning specialists

    3.____

4. Which of the following administration philosophies or strategies is part of the future-oriented trend in park and recreation management?

    A. Planning programs with the staff, chiefly by updating past programs
    B. Evaluating outcomes primarily through attendance figures
    C. Providing programs and services based on social and economic needs of the community
    D. Requiring financial accountability and justifying budgets based on historical precedent

    4.____

5. The _____ approach to leisure service sees recreation as an important community service that is carried on both for its own sake and because it contributes to the mental and physical health of participants.

    A. human-services   B. prescriptive
    C. environmental   D. quality-of-life

    5.____

6. More or increased _____ is NOT a growing trend in leisure services.

    A. centralized personnel structure
    B. emphasis on health and fitness

    6.____

C. consideration of leisure's contribution to quality of life
D. emphasis on noncompetitive forms of play

7. The MOST common means of financing public recreation and park departments is through

    A. bonds
    B. grants
    C. taxes
    D. fees and charges

8. For evaluating the effectiveness of specific programs offered by a park and recreation department, each of the following methods is commonly used EXCEPT

    A. systems-based, goal-achievement models
    B. internal auditing by top management
    C. staff-based evaluation processes
    D. participant-based evaluation

9. A public agency that favors the delegation of authority is BEST described as

    A. heterogeneous
    B. decentralized
    C. individualistic
    D. irresponsible

10. The ability to _____ is NOT generally considered to be a core process that an entry-level employee in a park and recreation department should master.

    A. carry out both program planning and organizational planning
    B. formally articulate resource needs
    C. utilize leadership processes
    D. teach

11. A _____ budget is designed in such a way that large units of work, or special programs, are isolated, identified, and described in detail.

    A. object classification
    B. function classification
    C. program
    D. performance

12. When programming recreational activities for participants in middle childhood (6-12 years), it is important to remember that they are generally

    A. preferring separation into sexually segregated groups
    B. physically aggressive
    C. physically growing more quickly than in preschool years
    D. unconcerned about ideas such as competence, achievement, and approval from others

13. Of the following issues, _____ is LEAST likely to be negotiated in a park and recreation labor union contractual agreement.

    A. work hours
    B. contracting work, or *outsourcing*
    C. safety regulations
    D. retirement plans

14. Which of the following is considered to be the responsibility of an auxiliary staff member at a park and recreation department?

    A. Supervision of sport programs
    B. Monitoring adherence to agency rules
    C. Direction of administrative guidelines
    D. Organizing sport activities

15. Traditionally, leisure facilities have been planned according to

    A. concepts of the neighborhood and community
    B. urban planning methods based on land-use principles
    C. a needs index
    D. recommended standards of open space

16. Public agencies such as park and recreation departments typically use one of several contemporary models in evaluating whether the agency has achieved its stated objectives. Which of the following is NOT one of these models?
    Evaluation designed to measure the

    A. overall quality of programs, based on the opinion of an advisory board
    B. effectiveness of programs in meeting their stated goals and objectives
    C. effectiveness of personnel in carrying out stated program goals and objectives
    D. level of satisfaction of program participants

17. It is NOT typically a function of a public park and recreation agency's board or commission to

    A. review and approve all policies and work with the agency's managers to develop plans for meeting present and future leisure needs of the community
    B. consider and approve all personnel appointments or promotions
    C. articulate to the agency's director and staff how the details of administration should be carried out
    D. carry out long-range planning in cooperation with other community organizations to meet public recreational needs

18. In handling employment inquiries, application forms, and interviews for employment, questions to the applicant about _____ may be allowed under law, whether their use is job-related or not.

    A. employment history
    B. physical requirements
    C. arrest and conviction record
    D. age

19. According to most current practices in public agencies, any overspending or underspending in the year's budget is to be brought to the department head's attention in the month of

    A. January   B. February
    C. March or April   D. November

20. In order to avoid legal liability for certain activities involving children, some park and recreation departments use the convention of permission slips signed by a parent or guardian, in which they are asked to waive the right to sue in case of injury or accident. For several reasons, these slips offer the department a false sense of security. Which of the following is NOT one of these reasons? 20.___
    I. In all cases, signed statements are invalid if the risks of the activity are not understood.
    II. The waiver is not valid unless signed by both parents, no matter what their geographic location.
    III. They cannot waive the right of a child to bring suit against the agency when the child reaches the legal age for doing so.

    The CORRECT answer is:

    A. I *only*   B. I, II   C. I, III   D. I, II, III

21. Which of the following recreation facilities would most likely be located at or near the intersection of major or secondary thoroughfares near the center of a 4- or 5-square mile service area? 21.___

    A. Playlot   B. Large park
    C. Playground   D. Athletic field

22. Which of the following is NOT a level of planning commonly associated with recreation and park facilities? 22.___

    A. Planning that focuses solely on recreation and park development within a total community, sometimes as a separate portion of a total plan
    B. Regional planning that takes into account services and facilities offered by adjacent jurisdictions
    C. Planning that is concerned with the development of a particular facility or the needs of a single neighborhood
    D. Total master planning that considers all aspects of municipal growth, including industrial and residential development, transportation, education, housing, health, etc.

23. The MAIN advantage of a structured, centralized approach to recreational programming is 23.___

    A. being able to respond to local neighborhood needs
    B. optimum legal protection from liability claims
    C. more efficient use of personnel resources
    D. a set of clear-cut standards for fulfilling the agency's stated objectives

24. When programming recreational activities for participants in middle adulthood (40-65 years), it is important to remember that they generally 24.___

    A. experience physiological changes in the brain
    B. begin to experience instability in cognitive skills
    C. display a loss of creativity
    D. tend to gain weight easily

25. In park and recreation accounting, concurrent auditing represents 25.____
    A. a preaudit of expected income or disbursements
    B. a formal check of specific administrative or program divisions of a department, or construction or maintenance projects
    C. a form of bookkeeping report showing the assets and liabilities of a given fund or budget
    D. all departmental expenditures that have been authorized and carried out

KEY (CORRECT ANSWERS)

1.	B	11.	C
2.	C	12.	A
3.	A	13.	B
4.	C	14.	A
5.	D	15.	C
6.	A	16.	A
7.	C	17.	C
8.	B	18.	A
9.	B	19.	B
10.	B	20.	C

21. D
22. B
23. D
24. D
25. A

TEST 2

DIRECTIONS: Each question or incomplete statement is followed by several suggested answers or completions. Select the one that BEST answers the question or completes the statement. *PRINT THE LETTER OF THE CORRECT ANSWER IN THE SPACE AT THE RIGHT.*

1. Each of the following is a benefit associated with the use of a *matrix* structure in a public park and recreation department EXCEPT

    A. greater opportunity of employees' personal development
    B. better technical performance
    C. improved flexibility in conditions of change and uncertainty
    D. involvement in long-range planning of employees at every level

    1.___

2. Which of the following statements about recreationists in early adulthood (20-39 years) is generally TRUE?

    A. They are more self-centered than adolescents.
    B. Their friendships are characterized by less intimacy.
    C. They experience a lack of stability in intellectual skills.
    D. They expand their social relationships through new contacts within the occupational and community settings.

    2.___

3. When programming recreation activities, an administrator's choices are likely to be affected by each of the following factors EXCEPT

    A. the number of potential activities
    B. the characteristics of participants
    C. the funds required
    D. personnel

    3.___

4. A recreation programmer wants to stage a single-elimination summer softball tournament at the department's facilities. Each of the following is an advantage associated with the single-elimination format EXCEPT it

    A. is usually more interesting for spectators
    B. may accommodate a large number of participants
    C. encourages maximum participation
    D. is the most economical to conduct

    4.___

5. In a recreation or park facility's off-season, an administrator wants to maintain a minimum level of care. Typically, how often should litter at the facility be picked up?

    A. Daily   B. Weekly
    C. Monthly   D. Every two months

    5.___

6. Funding agencies for public park and recreation departments have historically applied strict criteria for determining grant recipients. Which of the following statements about their considerations is generally FALSE?

    A. There must be evidence that existing programs and facilities are being fully utilized.
    B. Agencies applying for grants must be prepared to guarantee a substantial portion of the total grant proposal.

    6.___

C. Higher priority is given to proposals that come from more than one agency or sponsor.
D. Wherever possible, grant proposals should be designed to serve the general population, rather than isolated or special-need communities.

7. In public recreation programs, sport accounts for about _____% of all active involvement.

    A. 10-30 B. 35-50 C. 60-75 D. 80-95

8. Which of the following is NOT a level of responsibility defined by the functional classification of personnel analysis?

    A. Managerial B. Tutorial
    C. Logistical D. Operational

9. During a community needs assessment, a park and recreation department would most likely conduct use surveys among the community members in order to determine the _____ leisure needs of the community.

    A. expressed B. normative C. relative D. perceived

10. The main disadvantage to using an *object classification* type of budget for a park and recreation department is that

    A. it does not relate expenditures meaningfully to programs
    B. certain expenditures, such as personnel, are not considered *objects*
    C. it does not provide complete itemization of expenditures
    D. it does not take unplanned expenditures into account

11. Which of the following is NOT a guideline to follow in preparing a newspaper release for a public park and recreation department event or service?

    A. The release should stick to the facts and avoid editorializing.
    B. An attempt should be made to feature a prominent or interesting individual or group of people in the article.
    C. The most important information should be included at the beginning of the article.
    D. The release should be limited to 2 or 3 pages.

12. In a public school or college's recreational facilities, the priority of use must be

    A. intramural or campus recreational programming
    B. intercollegiate practice sessions or competition
    C. formal academic program use
    D. community residents

13. For a supervisor in a park and recreation department, each of the following is a guideline to follow in taking disciplinary action with employees EXCEPT

    A. when correction is required, it should be handled in private
    B. the worker should be told what he or she can do to correct the situation
    C. the action should not be taken until some time after the need for it has been established
    D. take the same corrective actions for the same behaviors with different individuals

14. The healthiest way a park and recreation department manager can approach the subject of inter-employee conflict is to view it as

    A. inevitable, but desirable and able to be used to constructive ends
    B. a healthy sign that workers in the department intend to challenge and compete with one another to meet departmental goals
    C. an inevitable product of a close working relationship that should be not denied, but endured peaceably
    D. a harmful and destructive influence that should be avoided at all costs

15. Which of the following is NOT generally considered to be a guideline to follow in determining when, and for what, recreation fees and charges are justified?

    A. Frequently charge where *preservation* is the dominant function
    B. Be sure that some benefit accrues to the taxpayer
    C. The specific services to be charged for and the fee should be matters of local choice
    D. Frequently charge where *use* is the dominant function

16. Generally, which of the following approaches to urban planning is used LEAST often?

    A. Developing an ideal model of the community
    B. Cost-revenue model
    C. User-oriented approach
    D. Needs index model

17. When conditions within a working group are only moderately favorable or unfavorable (i.e., the leader is well-liked but the task under consideration is unstructured), what type of leadership style is most appropriate?

    A. Laissez-faire   B. Task-oriented
    C. Authoritarian   D. Relationship-oriented

18. In a park and recreation department, a cost-benefit analysis is LEAST likely to be useful for

    A. identifying high- and low-cost programs and services as related to maintenance, administration, and direct leadership costs per participant-hour of service rendered
    B. providing valuable support data for justifying budget requests
    C. providing essential data for determining the cost-effectiveness of individual department personnel
    D. permitting the assignment of priorities to specific programs and services

19. In recent years, the number of volunteers working for public park and recreation departments has increased among certain segments of the population. Among the following groups, which has shown the LEAST significant increase in volunteer service?

    A. Females   B. Males
    C. Poor people   D. Minorities

20. The major type of legislation affecting parks and recreation is the

    A. regulatory law   B. special district law
    C. enabling law   D. home rule legislation

21. When programming recreational activities for participants in late adulthood (over 65 years), it is important to remember that they generally

 A. do not require a significant restructuring of time
 B. have a self-concept that tends to be more dependent upon external factors
 C. prefer to live in close contact with others of their age group
 D. become less active if they are men, and more active if they are women

22. The self-study approach to agency evaluation, outlined by the National Recreation and Park Association, includes standards that are used in measuring the effectiveness of a department in several major categories. Which of the following is NOT one of these categories?

 A. Administration B. Evaluation
 C. Programming   D. Funding

23. Decisions made at the lower level of an agency's management, which are part of operational planning and program implementation, are described as _____ decisions.

 A. primary   B. problem-oriented
 C. reflex   D. task-oriented

24. In park and recreation applications, a *flowchart* is used to

 A. view the community-wide availability of programs and detect under- or over-provision of different types of activities on a geographical basis
 B. show all events or continuing activities in a convenient and easily understood form
 C. show individual projects or programs laid out along a calendar, with specific tasks indicated for the dates on which they are to be begun and completed
 D. identify major facilities and ongoing programs

25. In recreation and sports injury cases involving parents and children, the parents, but not the child, can be barred from recovery for a child's injury under certain conditions. Which of the following is NOT one of these conditions?
 The

 A. parent has failed to exercise reasonable care to prevent the child from placing himself in a situation in which lack of self-protective capacity may reasonably be expected to result in harm to the child
 B. child is too young to exercise self-protection
 C. child's incapacity is a contributing factor in harm
 D. injury involves an *attractive nuisance*

KEY (CORRECT ANSWERS)

1.	D	11.	D
2.	D	12.	C
3.	A	13.	C
4.	C	14.	A
5.	A	15.	A
6.	D	16.	B
7.	C	17.	D
8.	B	18.	C
9.	D	19.	A
10.	A	20.	C

21. D
22. D
23. D
24. C
25. D

EXAMINATION SECTION
TEST 1

DIRECTIONS: Each question or incomplete statement is followed by several suggested answers or completions. Select the one that BEST answers the question or completes the statement. *PRINT THE LETTER OF THE CORRECT ANSWER IN THE SPACE AT THE RIGHT.*

1. A well-conceived and effectively presented budget should do each of the following EXCEPT

    A. inform taxpayers and government officials of the amounts of money spent, the sources of revenue, and the costs of achieving departmental goals
    B. serve for evaluating the program and ensuring that objectives are met
    C. help in promoting flexible operational procedures by creating very few classifications for all expenditures, and requiring flexible procedures for approving them
    D. provide a general statement of the financial needs, resources, and plans of the department, including an outline of all program elements and their costs and allocations for facilities and personnel

2. Among volunteers who offer time to park and recreation departments, which of the following motivating factors is most prevalent?

    A. Preparation for paid employment
    B. Family influences
    C. A desire to feel needed
    D. A desire to be helpful

3. Which of the following approaches to leisure service is found chiefly among recreation and park managers who serve in resource-based agencies?

    A. Individualist
    B. Prescriptive
    C. Environmental/aesthetic
    D. Human-services

4. In most public park and recreation departments, the largest area of use for volunteer workers is in

    A. direct leadership of groups or assisting professional leaders at work
    B. specialized educational appointments
    C. clerical assistance and helping with mailings, reports, and similar assignments
    D. administrative, promotional, or advisory activities

5. The use of night lighting at outdoor recreational facilities typically creates each of the following benefits EXCEPT

    A. deterring personal crime
    B. overall lower cost per hour of public use
    C. beautification of the park by enhancing plants, trees, and architectural features
    D. distinguishing activities within the park

6. Of the four types of in-service training administered to entry-level park and recreation employees, which is most likely to be delivered on an individual basis?

A. General career development
B. Training to keep the worker up to date
C. Orientation to the job
D. Training related specifically to the position for which the employee was selected

7. In recent years, community leisure-service organizations have adopted each of the following methods for achieving a high degree of productivity and efficiency EXCEPT

   A. cost-cutting practices
   B. zero-based budgeting
   C. a more extensive use of cost-benefit analysis
   D. reduced contracting, concession, and leasing arrangements

8. Which of the following statements concerning contributory negligence and children is TRUE?
   A child
   I. under 7 years of age is conclusively adjudged to be incapable of contributory negligence
   II. between 7 and 10 years of age is rebuttably presumed to be incapable of negligence
   III. over fourteen years of age is presumed capable of negligence

   The CORRECT answer is:

   A. I only   B. I, II   C. I, III   D. II, III

9. In general, a daily program schedule is divided into blocks of time, with major blocks of time of an hour or more per block incorporated. Generally, the daily program schedule is arranged with

   A. one block of time scheduled in the morning and one in the afternoon
   B. one in the morning and two in the afternoon
   C. only one major block per day, usually in the morning
   D. only one major block per day, usually in the afternoon

10. The MAIN advantage of an unstructured, decentralized approach to recreational programming is

    A. being able to respond to local neighborhood needs and special characteristics
    B. a set of core activities that meet clear program guidelines
    C. more intimate contact between community members and recreational leaders
    D. more efficient use of personnel resources

11. According to the Management-by-Objectives model (MBO), which of the following is NOT a guideline for the setting of park and recreation agency objectives?

    A. Objectives must be broad and open to interpretation by evaluators.
    B. Personnel at each level should play a role in setting their own objectives.
    C. A limited number of major objectives should be used for each unit or individual.
    D. Each objective should be given a precise time limit for accomplishment.

12. Which of the following steps in the purchasing process of a public agency would typically occur FIRST?   12.____

    A. Justification   B. Bids
    C. Specifications   D. Purchase orders

13. Of the various types of fees and charges at their disposal, public recreation and park departments most often use   13.____

    A. entrance/admission fees   B. lease revenue
    C. program/activity fees   D. rental fees

14. When a park and recreation official has the opportunity to speak with the media about the operations of the department, he or she should   14.____

    A. speak in 30-second quotes, or shorter
    B. use technical language that will show the significance of the project or organization
    C. dress in bright colors
    D. use preface remarks

15. Each of the following is an advantage associated with contracting out various functions of a public park and recreation department EXCEPT   15.____

    A. greater departmental independence
    B. avoiding the restrictions of bureaucratic structures and similar political institutions
    C. lower personnel costs
    D. clearer contractual specification of quantity, quality, and price of work

16. Which of the following is NOT a growing trend in the personnel assignment policies of larger park and recreation departments?   16.____

    A. Having a fixed number of full-time, year-round employees supplemented by a limited number of specialists during the year, and an influx of summer workers for playground or camping programs
    B. Greater responsibility of *face-to-face* leaders in coordinating and directing programs
    C. Assignment of leaders to other district- or city-wide roles which can be carried out during slack periods
    D. Rotation of assignments at different seasons

17. According to most current practices in public agencies, the first work sessions on the departmental budget for the following year are generally held in the months of   17.____

    A. March-April   B. May-June
    C. August-September   D. October-November

18. Which of the following appears to have the LEAST significant effect on a person's opportunities to engage in recreational activities?   18.____

    A. Time
    B. Geographic and environmental resources
    C. Motivation
    D. Health and fitness

4 (#1)

19. A park and recreation department's _____ is a document that includes planned and proposed expenditures for carrying out major purchases and construction projects of a substantial and long-term nature.

   A. operating budget
   B. balance sheet
   C. capital budget
   D. performance budget

20. A large park of several hundred acres will generally provide _____ acres of area for every user.

   A. 1-2   B. 5   C. 10   D. 20

21. Concerning intramural and extramural sports programs, most park and recreation departments have specific policies designed to deal with the issue of forfeited contests. Which of the following is NOT generally one of these policies?

   A. A team or individual not ready to play within thirty minutes after the scheduled time is charged with a forfeit.
   B. An individual or team may be assessed a forfeit fee.
   C. Two forfeits result in the elimination of an individual or team from all further participation in that sport.
   D. If a team or individual leaves before the forfeit is duly noted by an official or supervisor, then both teams should be charged with a forfeit.

22. Most local park and recreation agencies function within a framework of legislation provided by the

   A. federal government
   B. state government
   C. municipal government
   D. appointed board

23. Within a working group assigned to a specific task, the task structure is measured by each of the following EXCEPT the degree to which

   A. members understand what the goal is
   B. the correctness of a decision can be demonstrated by authority or logic
   C. multiple paths to the goal are evident
   D. one solution is more correct

24. During a summer recreation program, quiet activities are usually BEST scheduled for

   A. as late in the day as possible
   B. the early afternoon
   C. mid-day
   D. the early morning

25. Which of the following statements about adolescent recreationists is FALSE?

   A. They generally show a rapid increase in lung capacity.
   B. They are capable not only of describing, but of explaining situations or phenomena.
   C. Norms for male or female behavior are generally discovered through interactions with the opposite sex.
   D. They are concerned with the meaning of life according to religious and philosophical perspectives.

KEY (CORRECT ANSWERS)

1.	C	11.	A
2.	D	12.	A
3.	C	13.	C
4.	A	14.	A
5.	B	15.	A
6.	C	16.	A
7.	D	17.	B
8.	C	18.	C
9.	B	19.	C
10.	A	20.	B

21.	A
22.	B
23.	C
24.	C
25.	C

TEST 2

DIRECTIONS: Each question or incomplete statement is followed by several suggested answers or completions. Select the one that BEST answers the question or completes the statement. *PRINT THE LETTER OF THE CORRECT ANSWER IN THE SPACE AT THE RIGHT.*

1. In developing any recreation program, an administrator's primary emphasis is nearly always on

    A. education for leisure
    B. providing organized or supervised activities
    C. coordinating and assisting functions
    D. providing facilities for unscheduled and unsupervised use

2. Each of the following is a disadvantage associated with the use of air-supported structures as a housing for recreational facilities EXCEPT

    A. their susceptibility to vandalism
    B. their short life expectancy
    C. lack of flexibility in yearly program scheduling
    D. possible zoning law conflicts

3. Typically, which of the following would be the final step in the development of a maintenance management plan for a recreational facility?
   The

    A. definition of the maintenance plan's overall goals and objectives
    B. development of work order request forms for non-routine, nonrecurring maintenance tasks
    C. creation of a format for scheduling maintenance work
    D. development of a form for daily maintenance work and assignments

4. In liability terms, each of the following is a means of risk reduction for a park and recreation department EXCEPT

    A. conducting periodic safety inspections for all facilities and equipment
    B. training all employees in safety practices, first aid, and preventive maintenance
    C. clearly labeling potential risks to users
    D. developing safety rules for the operation of facilities and equipment

5. Managing a public park and recreation department like a business, using marketing strategies, has proven effective for many departments in trimming costs and streamlining services, but the marketing approach does have several disadvantages. Which of the following is NOT generally considered to be one of them?

    A. The bottom line of program development is profitability.
    B. Efforts at securing public subsidies are likely to be reduced.
    C. Services to poorer community residents may atrophy.
    D. Possible ventures may be evaluated only in terms of who will be able to pay for them.

6. The need for public relations in the field of parks and recreation is enforced by certain prevailing public attitudes. Which of the following is NOT generally considered to be one of these prevailing attitudes?

   A. Frequent occasions, brought about by the very nature of park and recreation operations, when individual citizens become irritated, frustrated, or disappointed
   B. Limited knowledge of the range of services and programs offered
   C. A generalized opposition to public funding of a department that is not considered to be part of the infrastructure
   D. The feeling that public recreation is not really a necessity; that the public is able to meet its leisure needs independently

7. In most states, the statute of limitations for litigating actions involving negligence is

   A. 1 year
   B. 2 years
   C. 10 years
   D. in most states, there is no statute of limitations

8. In park and recreation management applications, a *diagraph* is used to

   A. view the community-wide availability of programs and detect under- or over-provision of different types of activities on a geographical basis
   B. show all events or continuing activities in a convenient and easily understood form
   C. show individual projects or programs laid out along a calendar, with specific tasks indicated for the dates on which they are to be begun and completed
   D. identify major facilities and ongoing programs

9. Which of the following is considered to be the responsibility of a program-administrative staff member at a park and recreation department?

   A. Monitoring personnel practices
   B. Preparing statistical or analytical reports of operations
   C. Monitoring facility use and operations
   D. Implementing policies for safety

10. The probationary period for most newly-hired park and recreation personnel is

    A. 24-48 hours
    B. 4-6 weeks
    C. 3-6 months
    D. 1-2 years

11. For busy community members who have fluctuating schedules, and who want to compete in a more structured competitive environment, a recreation and park department's most effective way of dealing with competitive sports such as tennis is to establish a _____ tournament structure for participants.

    A. single elimination
    B. double elimination
    C. challenge
    D. round-robin

12. A specific tax leveled against the assessed value of residential or industrial property, the amount of which is assigned directly to the public park and recreation fund and used exclusively for that purpose, is known as a(n) _____ tax.

    A. millage
    B. real estate
    C. impact
    D. levy

13. A _____ approach to leisure service sees recreation not as an activity carried on for its own sake, but as designed to accomplish specific therapeutic goals.

    A. human-services   B. marketing
    C. individualist   D. prescriptive

14. Which of the following steps in the development of a park and recreation program is typically administered first?

    A. Establishing goals, objectives, and policies
    B. Identifying the range of possible activities and services
    C. Assessing participant or community needs and interests
    D. Developing a program plan

15. The growing trend in park and recreation departmental budgeting is toward the use of _____ budgets.

    A. program   B. function classification
    C. performance   D. line-item

16. What type of accounting system shows, on updated expenditure reports, all encumbrances or charges against specified accounts?

    A. Balance sheet   B. Concurrent auditing
    C. Work program auditing   D. Accrual

17. Which of the following statements about recreationists in middle childhood (6-12 years) is generally TRUE?

    A. Their muscles develop in function, but are still immature in size and strength.
    B. They have not mastered the concept of numbers, clock time, or calendar time.
    C. They do not exhibit abstract thought processes.
    D. They know rules which specify right from wrong, but may not understand the reasoning behind them.

18. Which of the following is NOT a typical benefit associated with informal structures and processes within the framework of a park and recreation department?

    A. Enhancement of a manager's authority
    B. Reduced time requirements for developing projects
    C. Increased opportunity for lower-level personnel to share meaningfully in agency planning
    D. Improved planning and problem-solving functions

19. Which of the following administration philosophies or strategies is NOT part of the future-oriented trend in park and recreation management?

    A. Evaluating services in terms of human consequences
    B. Offering programs anywhere in the community, with staff resources helping residents develop their own leadership skills
    C. Funding all basic programs from tax allocations
    D. Acting in an enabling or catalyzing role in matching community resources to citizen's needs

20. When a recreation and park manager has news of interest to the local newspaper, there are several approaches he or she might take. Which of the following should be used most sparingly?

    A. Arranging a news conference and invite interested reporters and editors
    B. Calling the newspaper, summarizing the information briefly to the appropriate editor or reporter, and allowing the person to suggest a course of action
    C. Writing the information in the form of a *letter to the editor* and mail or deliver it to the editor
    D. Preparing a news release and mail or deliver it to the editor

21. Each of the following is a typical policy used by park and recreation departments concerning the reservation of recreational facilities by community members EXCEPT

    A. cancellations must be made in person with the proper identification
    B. cancellations must be made 24 hours in advance, or a no-show penalty will apply
    C. persons absent 10 minutes past the reserved time forfeit all rights to the facility
    D. reservations must be made at least 4 hours in advance

22. In a departmental budget, the function of a work program is *primarily* to

    A. determine scheduling needs for the coming year
    B. estimate personnel expenditures
    C. establish a clear set of administrative performance standards
    D. outline tasks to be performed, standards of service and efficiency, and methods to be used

23. While conducting a needs assessment of the community, park and recreation administrators relate the leisure services currently offered to a set of national standards for such services in similar communities. In this situation, the administration is determining the community's _____ need for services.

    A. expressed   B. normative
    C. perceived   D. relative

24. Which of the following is not typically a heading used on a written maintenance plan for a recreational facility?

    A. Personnel   B. Chain of command
    C. Maintenance standards D. Frequency

25. According to the established national standard, a park and recreation manager who is planning a leisure facility should rely upon the figure of 1 acre of land needed for every _____ community residents.

    A. 100   B. 800   C. 1200   D. 2500

KEY (CORRECT ANSWERS)

1.	D	11.	C
2.	C	12.	A
3.	B	13.	D
4.	C	14.	C
5.	B	15.	A
6.	C	16.	D
7.	B	17.	D
8.	B	18.	A
9.	A	19.	C
10.	C	20.	A

21. D
22. D
23. B
24. B
25. B

EXAMINATION SECTION
TEST 1

DIRECTIONS: Each question or incomplete statement is followed by several suggested answers or completions. Select the one that BEST answers the question or completes the statement. *PRINT THE LETTER OF THE CORRECT ANSWER IN THE SPACE AT THE RIGHT.*

1. The basic design of neighborhood playgrounds provides for a variety of separate areas. The LARGEST of these areas in a neighborhood playground is that generally set aside for use by

    A. little children and their guardians
    B. older children, teenagers, and young adults
    C. older people (senior citizens)
    D. physically active and mature adults

    1._____

2. If a general park foreman is vague and indefinite in assigning to employees responsibilities for various phases of work, the MOST important consequence of this is likely to be

    A. a shift in lines of authority within the organization
    B. friction, misunderstanding, and ineffective work
    C. that certain more aggressive individuals will assume responsibility in order to get the work done
    D. the unsupervised and unplanned training of individuals in assuming responsibility

    2._____

3. Present recreation programs must be expanded to provide a progression of sports competition.
   According to a park department report, the PRINCIPAL reason for this expanded program is the need to

    A. channel the naturally aggressive inclinations of youngsters into wholesome physical exercise and rivalry
    B. enable qualified, eligible city youths to achieve success in professional athletic activity
    C. make the fullest possible use of presently existing facilities
    D. provide the means for improving the physical fitness of male youths as a factor in national defense

    3._____

4. Aside from the requirements of law, the BASIC reason why the park department publishes periodic reports should be to

    A. emphasize the need for additional funds if it is to perform its work adequately
    B. help the public gain an understanding of its program and to try to enlist public support
    C. point up the present efficiency and the expanding responsibilities of the park department
    D. show just how the park department uses the funds it is allotted in its budget

    4._____

5. If a supervising park foreman assigns an assistant gardener to temporarily supervise a group of seasonal employees, it would be MOST important for the general park foreman to describe carefully to the assistant gardener

    5._____

A. the educational and work background of each of the seasonal employees involved
B. the length of time the assignment is likely to last
C. the nature and extent of the supervisory duties to be assumed
D. why seasonal employees are never as industrious as regular employees

6. As stated in a park department publication, the prime concern of the park department must continue to be that of

   A. developing large-scale ocean and bay front bathing and boating facilities
   B. expanding the scope of operation and varieties of services of the city's cultural institutions
   C. meeting the recreational needs of senior citizens
   D. providing adequate recreational facilities in local areas

7. Requests for information from the comptroller about claims against the city arising from accidents in the parks sometimes concern the date of the request for repairs and the date of repairs.
   This information is important in such cases MAINLY because it

   A. indicates the claimant failed to use due care in the use of park facilities
   B. is an additional check on the operation of the main tenance forces
   C. may affect the liability of the city in the accident
   D. points up the shortage of personnel available to make repairs

8. It is important for a supervisor to take prompt action upon requests from subordinates MAINLY because

   A. delays in making decisions mean that they must then be made on the basis of facts which can no longer be up-to-date
   B. favorable action on such requests is more likely to result when a decision is made quickly
   C. it is an indication that the supervisor has his work well organized
   D. promptness in such matters helps maintain good employee morale

9. As a supervisor, you realize that your superior, when under pressure, has a habit of giving you oral orders which are not always clear and also lack sufficient detail. The BEST procedure for you to follow in such situations would be to

   A. obtain clarification by requesting needed details at the time you receive such orders
   B. consider past orders of a similar nature to determine the probable intent of your superior
   C. frequently consult your superior during the course of the job in order to secure the required details to complete the job
   D. request your superior to put all his orders to you in writing

10. Some supervisors have their subordinates meet with them in group discussions of troublesome problems.
    The MAIN advantage of such group discussions as a supervisory tool is that they can be directed toward the

    A. appraisal of the personalities involved
    B. development of new policies and regulations

C. circulation of new material and information
D. pooling of experience in the solution of common problems

11. The PRINCIPAL disadvantage of using form letters to reply to written complaints made by members of the park-using public is that such form letters

    A. tend to make any investigation of the original complaint rather superficial
    B. are limited by their design to handle only a few possible situations that could give rise to complaints
    C. lack the desirable element of the personal touch for the recipient
    D. tend to lose their effectiveness by quickly becoming obsolete

11.____

12. Below are repair items in a county staff inspection report of an inspection of a large recreation center made in mid-November.
    The item for which the target date would MOST probably read *at once* would be

    A. chip, red lead and paint wrought iron fence
    B. clean one filter in kitchen exhaust duct of Golden Age Center kitchen
    C. repair broken game tables
    D. replace corktiles on swimming pool wall

12.____

13. In a headquarters inspection report, the one of the following tasks whose accomplishment would MOST probably be the responsibility of the county director is

    A. accelerating repairs to gate hinges
    B. alerting local Police Precinct and Youth Squad of exceptional vandalism
    C. replacing missing privet along Avenue S
    D. studying removal of horseshoe courts and developing same as passive recreation area

13.____

14. According to the work count report, the one of the following work units which is measured in terms of area is

    A. catch basins - hand cleaned
    B. painting - wrought iron fencing
    C. paper picking
    D. sweeping mechanically

14.____

15. A helper who has been on the job for some time complains to a foreman that he is learning very little because the maintainer with whom he works does not explain anything. The FIRST thing the foreman should do is to

    A. tell the helper to make a formal written request for a transfer
    B. send a memo to his maintainers reminding them of their responsibility to train helpers
    C. discuss the problem privately with the maintainer in question
    D. tell the helper to learn as much as he can on his own

15.____

16. With respect to the city's employee grievance procedure, it would be MOST correct to state that

16.____

A. the commissioner of labor is the highest ranking official, excepting the judge, who can be involved in a particular grievance
B. the person with the grievance has the right to be represented by virtually anyone he chooses
C. the one having the grievance (the grievant) can be represented by the majority organization only if he is a member thereof
D. time limits are not set concerning adjudication in order to insure the fullest consideration of the particular grievance

17. According to the rules and regulations of the department of parks, loitering or remaining in any park without general or special permission from the park commissioner is prohibited between

    A. 12:00 P.M. and sunrise
    B. 11:00 P.M. and one-half hour before sunrise
    C. 12:00 midnight and one-half hour before sunrise
    D. three hours after sunset and one-half hour before sunrise

18. According to the rules and regulations of the department of parks, when a sidewalk fronts on the roadway of a park-street, dust from such sidewalk may

    A. be swept into the gutter before nine o'clock in the morning
    B. be swept into the gutter, and there piled, before the first sweeping of the roadway of the park-street by the street cleaners
    C. be swept into the gutter in neat piles at any reasonable time if not so piled as to constitute a traffic hazard or health menace
    D. never be swept into the gutter

19. According to the rules and regulations of the department of parks, any violation of the rules and regulations

    A. is punishable by not more than 60 days imprisonment
    B. is punishable by a fine of not more than 100 dollars
    C. shall be deemed to be a misdemeanor unless otherwise so designated by the trial judge or the rules and regulations
    D. shall be triable by a city magistrate

20. According to the rules and regulations of the department of parks, possession in parks of merchandise in quantities, packages or containers customarily associated with peddling shall be deemed to be _____ evidence of offering for sale.

    A. circumstantial   B. conclusive
    C. presumptive   D. prima facie

21. According to the rules and regulations of the department of parks, unless duly licensed by the park commissioner, no person shall bring beer, ale or other alcoholic beverages into any park

    A. at any time
    B. except on legal holidays
    C. in containers having a capacity of more than a quart
    D. when the bottle, flask, or container thereof has been opened prior to entering upon park property

22. Select the one of the following which is untrue according to the rules and regulations   22.____
    of the department of parks:

    A. Instruction in operating automobiles or motorcycles is permitted in certain areas of
       parks and park-streets if a prior permit has been granted by the park commissioner
    B. Invalid wheelchairs may be pushed along a boardwalk or a pedestrian walk without
       a license from the park commissioner
    C. In no case is cruising by a taxi in a park permitted
    D. Persons may push bicycles in a single file in a park to a place in a park designated
       for riding such bicycles

23. Our public city playgrounds fall into five general classifications.   23.____
    Select the one of the following which is NOT one of these five classifications:

    A. Neighborhood   B. Marginal
    C. School   D. Shoestring

24. Parkway gasoline service stations differ from other concessions in the park department   24.____
    with respect to the manner in which such concessionaires are selected MAINLY because
    such parkway gasoline service station concessions are granted on the basis of

    A. potential ability to operate successfully
    B. competitive bidding
    C. demonstrated experience
    D. financial responsibility

25. When two men are carrying a long object such as a plank, the one of the following which   25.____
    is LEAST important from a safety standpoint is that the

    A. load should be put down at the same time by both men
    B. two men should be of the same height
    C. two men should be in step
    D. plank should be carried on the same shoulder, that is right or left, of each man

26. Injuries are frequently caused when a workman, in lifting a heavy object, bends his back   26.____
    rather than bending his knees and, at the same time, keeping his back straight. Such
    injuries USUALLY result from pressure on the

    A. arms and shoulders
    B. collar bone and upper vertebrae (spine)
    C. lower spine
    D. ribs

27. A ten-year analysis of the major causes of fire, conducted fairly recently by the National   27.____
    Board of Fire Under writers, showed that of the following, the one that caused the HIGH-
    EST percentage of fires was

    A. matches and smoking
    B. misuse of electricity
    C. spontaneous combustion
    D. stoves, furnaces, and defective chimneys

28. In painting operations, the costs are generally about _____ labor, _____ paint.   28.____

    A. 50%; 50%   B. 60%; 40%   C. 70%; 30%   D. 80%; 20%

29. There are two distinct types of reel type lawn mowers–the *side wheel* drive and the *rear wheel* drive.
The one of the following concerning these two types of mowers which is TRUE is that

    A. a side wheel mower is usually faster than the rear wheel mower
    B. on the side wheel mower, the wheels generally operate within the width of the cutting unit
    C. the side wheel mower generally permits closer trimming next to walls or obstructions than the rear wheel mower
    D. the side wheel mower usually has a narrower wheel base than the rear wheel mower

30. The fuel mixture in a high production professional chain saw is usually _____ gasoline and _____ oil.

    A. high octane; detergent
    B. high octane; non-detergent
    C. regular; detergent
    D. regular; non-detergent

31. A windrow deflector on a large power mower would be designed MAINLY to

    A. enable the machine to follow ground contours easily
    B. permit a very small turning radius
    C. prevent compaction of the turf
    D. scatter clippings uniformly

32. On a *Toro Professional Mower* with a 3 unit assembly, the one of the following which is CLOSEST to the operator's seat is the

    A. choke   B. oil bath air cleaner
    C. reel clutch control D. roller bracket

33. Concerning the air cleaner on the *Whirlwind Model GK-Rotary-Scythe,* it would be MOST accurate to state that

    A. after it is cleaned, the air cleaner should be filled with fresh motor oil and gasoline
    B. the filter element should be soaked in gasoline
    C. it should be cleaned everytime the motor oil is changed
    D. the unit need not be dismantled in order to clean it

34. Concerning the motor lubrication of the ZIPPER 36" Sickle Bar Mower, it would be MOST accurate to state that the

    A. oil should be changed daily
    B. oil should be drained while motor is cool
    C. crankcase should be flushed when the oil is changed
    D. motor need not be stopped to check the oil level

35. In starting the motor of a *Gravely sickle and reel*, it would be MOST correct to state that

    A. before cranking motor the clutch levers should be in the middle position
    B. six or eight pulls on the starting strap are needed to start the motor
    C. the starting strap is wound counterclockwise around the lower fan pulley
    D. the throttle must be open all the way

36. If it is necessary to restore to its proper consistency white lead paint which has hardened due to cool weather, it is BEST to do this by

    A. the addition of boiled linseed oil
    B. the addition of turpentine
    C. vigorous stirring of the paint
    D. warming the paint

37. Bituminous surfaces often develop *map-cracked* surfaces which resemble boundary lines on maps.
    Such map-cracked areas on bituminous surfaces should be spot sealed

    A. any time of the year when the cracks are thoroughly dry
    B. only in the spring and during dry weather
    C. preferably in the summer and in rather warm weather
    D. any time of the year regardless of whether the cracks are wet or dry

38. According to generally accepted safety requirements and practices, the one of the following jobs that MUST be done under the supervision of the foreman of mechanics is

    A. applying boiler compound
    B. inspecting and recharging fire extinguishers
    C. lubricating unit heater motors
    D. lubricating vacuum pumps and motors

39. The knot that is USUALLY recommended for tying tools to be raised into a tree is a

    A. clove hitch
    B. figure of eight
    C. sheet bend
    D. square

40. The LARGEST individual item of expense in operating a public building is generally the cost of

    A. cleaning
    B. heating
    C. lighting
    D. repairing toilet plumbing

41. It is recommended that all tree-pruning wounds 3/4 inch or more in diameter be painted to protect the tree. The BEST paint to use, of the following, is

    A. a rubber base paint
    B. an alkyd resin paint
    C. emulsified asphalt
    D. red lead

42. With respect to lightning and trees, it would be MOST accurate to state that

    A. all species of trees appear to have the same susceptibility to attack by lightning
    B. lightning damage to tree root systems is rare
    C. the total damage done to a tree by a bolt of lightning is not always immediately apparent
    D. trees with shallow widespreading root systems are more liable to lightning injury than deep-rooted trees

43. An adequate supply of humus in the soil is one of the most important factors in a program of good soil management.
The one of the following statements about humus which is UNTRUE is that humus

    A. increases the water-holding capacity of soils
    B. modifies the soil structure
    C. readily absorbs the sun's rays
    D. retards the bacterial action in the soil to a very marked degree

44. The modern, widely available insect killers in common use fall MAINLY into three groups. The one of the following which is NOT one of these recognized groups is the

    A. botanicals
    B. chlorinated hydrocarbons
    C. cleaginous petroleums
    D. organic phosphates

45. Inorganic commercial fertilizers are the most common types used today. They are made in various mixtures. A 5-10-5 inorganic commercial fertilizer contains 5% _____, 10% _____, and 5% _____.

    A. nitrogen; phosphorous; potash
    B. nitrogen; potash; phosphorous
    C. nitrogen; potassium; potash
    D. phosphorous; nitrogen; potash

46. Against chewing insects such as caterpillars and beetles, it would be BEST to use a

    A. contact insecticide with a fine droplet mist or fog
    B. residual or surface insecticide in a coarser or wet spray
    C. space of knock-down insecticide in a coarser or wet spray
    D. space or knock-down insecticide with a fine droplet mist or fog

47. A hand-operated earth auger would be MOST likely used to

    A. cut weeds
    B. edge turf
    C. tamp sod
    D. test soil

48. In an inspection report, one of the items concerning a lawn area reads, *Fill in depression, grade, and embellish.* Embellish here means MOST NEARLY

    A. add fertilizer to
    B. improve the appearance of
    C. aerate
    D. roll

49. Areas shall be scarified manually until the surface is friable.
Friable in this sentence means MOST NEARLY

    A. easily crumbled into powder
    B. free of debris and organic matter
    C. free of rock
    D. raked evenly

50. To characterize a leaf as *serrated* means MOST NEARLY that the leaf

    A. is full of insects
    B. has an autumnal color
    C. has sawlike notches along the edge
    D. is semi-circular in shape

KEY (CORRECT ANSWERS)

1. B	11. C	21. C	31. D	41. C
2. B	12. B	22. A	32. C	42. C
3. A	13. D	23. D	33. C	43. D
4. B	14. C	24. B	34. A	44. C
5. C	15. C	25. B	35. A	45. A
6. D	16. B	26. C	36. D	46. B
7. C	17. C	27. A	37. D	47. D
8. D	18. B	28. D	38. A	48. B
9. A	19. D	29. A	39. A	49. A
10. D	20. D	30. D	40. A	50. C

EXAMINATION SECTION
TEST 1

DIRECTIONS: Each question or incomplete statement is followed by several suggested answers or completions. Select the one that BEST answers the question or completes the statement. *PRINT THE LETTER OF THE CORRECT ANSWER IN THE SPACE AT THE RIGHT.*

1. A maintenance man complains to you that he is getting all the boring jobs to do. You check and find that his complaint has no basis in fact.
   The one of the following which is the MOST likely reason why the maintenance man made such a claim is that he

   A. wants to get even with the supervisor
   B. lives in a world of fantasy
   C. believes the injustice to be real
   D. is jealous of other workers

   1.____

2. When on preliminary review of a mechanic's written grievance you feel the grievance to be unfounded, the FIRST step you should take is to

   A. show the mechanic where he is wrong
   B. check carefully to find out why the mechanic thinks that way
   C. try to humor the mechanic out of it
   D. tell the mechanic to stop complaining

   2.____

3. Assume that you decide to hold a private meeting with one of your mechanics who has a drinking problem that is affecting his work.
   At the meeting, the BEST way for you to handle this situation is to

   A. tell the mechanic off and then listen to what he has to say
   B. criticize the mechanic's behavior to get him to *open up* in order to help him correct his problem quickly
   C. try to get the mechanic to recognize his problem and find ways to solve it
   D. limit the discussion to matters concerning only the problem and look for immediate results

   3.____

4. The one of the following which is a generally accepted guide in criticizing a subordinate EFFECTIVELY is to

   A. criticize the improper act, not the individual
   B. put the listener on the defensive
   C. make the criticism general instead of specific
   D. correct the personality, not the situation

   4.____

5. The one of the following disciplinary methods by which you are MOST likely to be successful in getting a problem employee to improve his behavior is when you

   A. discipline the employee in front of others
   B. consider the matter to be ended after the disciplining
   C. give the exact same discipline no matter how serious the wrongdoing
   D. make an example of the employee

   5.____

73

6. Of the following statements, the one that is MOST applicable to a disciplinary situation is that discipline should be

   A. used after a cooling-off period
   B. identical for all employees
   C. consistent with the violation
   D. based on personal feelings

7. The one of the following approaches that is MOST important for you to take in evaluating a mechanic in order to increase his work productivity is to

   A. first have him evaluate his own performance
   B. meet with him to discuss how he is doing and what is expected on the job
   C. send him a copy of your evaluation of his work performance and give him the opportunity to submit written comments
   D. express in writing your appreciation of his work

8. Assume that you say to one of the mechanics, *Jim, that job you turned out today was top-notch. I didn't think you could do so well with the kind of material you had to work with.*
   This statement BEST describes an example of your

   A. recognition of the man's work
   B. disrespect for the man's feelings
   C. personal favoritism of the man
   D. constructive criticism of the man's work

9. In general, the OUTSTANDING characteristic of employees over 50 years of age is their

   A. resistance   B. endurance
   C. wisdom   D. job stability

10. You should be interested in the morale of your men because morale is MOST often associated with

    A. mechanization   B. automation
    C. production   D. seniority regulations

11. Assume that the maintenance work order system is about to be changed. Your workers would MOST likely show the LEAST resistance to this change if you

    A. downgrade the old maintenance work order system
    B. tell your workers how the change will benefit them
    C. post the notice of the change on the bulletin board
    D. tell the workers how the change will benefit management

12. Of the following, the BEST way to motivate a newly appointed mechanic is to

    A. explain the meaning of each assignment
    B. make the work more physically demanding
    C. test the mechanic's ability
    D. use as much authority as possible

13. The one of the following which is the LEAST important reason for giving employees information concerning policy changes which will affect them is that employees should know

    A. why the change is being made
    B. who will be affected by the change
    C. when the change will go into effect
    D. how much savings will be made by the change

14. A foreman who knows how to handle his men will MOST likely get them to produce more by treating them

    A. alike
    B. as individuals
    C. on a casual basis
    D. as a group

15. Of the following items, the one that a supervisor has the MOST right to expect from his employees is

    A. liking the job
    B. a fair day's work
    C. equal skill of all mechanics
    D. perfection

16. The one of the following which is the BEST practice for you to follow in handling a dispute between the workers is to

    A. side with one of the workers so as to end the dispute quickly
    B. pay no attention to the dispute and let the workers settle it themselves
    C. listen to each worker's story of the dispute and then decide how to settle it
    D. discuss the dispute with other workers and then decide how to settle it

17. You are likely to run into an employee morale problem when assigning a dirty job that comes up often.
    Of the following, the BEST method of assigning this work is to

    A. rotate this assignment
    B. assign it to the fastest worker
    C. assign it by seniority
    D. assign it to the least skilled worker

18. Of the following, the one that is generally regarded as the BEST aid to high work productivity of subordinates is a supervisor's skill in

    A. record keeping
    B. technical work
    C. setting up rules and regulations
    D. human relations

19. The BEST way to help a mechanic who comes to you for advice on a personal problem is to

    A. listen to the worker's problem without passing judgment
    B. tell the worker to forget about the problem and to stop letting it interfere with his work
    C. talk about your own personal problems to the worker
    D. mind your own business and leave the worker alone

20. You are in charge of the maintenance shop and have learned that within the next two weeks the maintenance shop will be moved to a new location on the plant grounds, but you have not learned why this move is taking place. Assume that you have decided not to keep this information from your mechanics until the reason is known but to inform them of this matter now.
Of the following, which one is the BEST argument that can be made regarding your decision?

    A. *Acceptable;* because although the reason is not now known, the mechanics will eventually find out about the move
    B. *Unacceptable;* because the mechanics do not know at this time the reason for the move and this will cause anxiety on their part
    C. *Acceptable*; because the mechanics will be affected by the move and they should be told what is happening
    D. *Unacceptable;* because the mechanics' advance knowledge of the move will tend to slow down their work output

21. Of the following, the FIRST action for a foreman to take in making a decision is to

    A. get all the facts
    B. develop alternate solutions
    C. get opinions of others
    D. know the results in advance

22. Assume that you have just been promoted to foreman.
Of the following, the BEST practice to follow regarding your previous experience at the mechanic's level is to

    A. continue to fraternize with your old friends
    B. use this experience to better understand those who now work for you
    C. use your old connections to keep top management informed of mechanics' views
    D. forget the mechanics' points of view

23. You have decided to hold regular group discussions with your subordinates on various aspects of their duties.
Of the following methods you might use to begin such a program, the one which is likely to be MOST productive is to

    A. express your own ideas and persuade the group to accept them
    B. save time and cover more ground by asking questions calling for yes or no answers
    C. propose to the group a general plan of action rather than specific ideas carefully worked out
    D. provide an informal atmosphere for the exchange of ideas

24. The principle of learning by which a foreman might get the BEST results in training his subordinates is:

    A. Letting the learner discover and correct his own mistakes
    B. Teaching the most technical part of the work first
    C. Teaching all parts of the work during the first training session
    D. Getting the learner to use as many of his five senses as possible

25. A new mechanic is to be trained to do an involved operation containing several steps of varying difficulty. This mechanic will MOST likely learn the operation more quickly if he is taught

    A. each step in its proper order
    B. the hardest steps first
    C. the easiest steps first
    D. first the steps that do not require tools

25.____

KEY (CORRECT ANSWERS)

1.	C	11.	B
2.	B	12.	A
3.	C	13.	D
4.	A	14.	B
5.	B	15.	B
6.	C	16.	C
7.	B	17.	A
8.	A	18.	D
9.	D	19.	A
10.	C	20.	C

21. A
22. B
23. D
24. D
25. C

TEST 2

DIRECTIONS: Each question or incomplete statement is followed by several suggested answers or completions. Select the one that BEST answers the question or completes the statement. *PRINT THE LETTER OF THE CORRECT ANSWER IN THE SPACE AT THE RIGHT.*

1. The one of the following job situations in which it is better to give a written order than an oral order is when

   A. the job involves many details
   B. you can check the job's progress easily
   C. the job is repetitive in nature
   D. there is an emergency

   1.___

2. Which one of the following serves as the BEST guideline for you to follow for effective written reports?
   Keep sentences

   A. short and limit sentences to one thought
   B. short and use as many thoughts as possible
   C. long and limit sentences to one thought
   D. long and use as many thoughts as possible

   2.___

3. Of the following, the BEST reason why a foreman generally should not do the work of an individual mechanic is that

   A. the shop's production figures will not be accurate
   B. a foreman is paid to supervise
   C. the foreman must maintain his authority
   D. the employee may become self-conscious

   3.___

4. One method by which a foreman might prepare written reports to management is to begin with the conclusions, results, or summary and to follow this with the supporting data.
   The BEST reason why management may prefer this form of report is because

   A. management lacks the specific training to understand the data
   B. the data completely supports the conclusions
   C. time is saved by getting to the conclusions of the report first
   D. the data contains all the information that is required for making the conclusions

   4.___

5. Forms used for time records and work orders are important to the work of a foreman PRIMARILY because they give him

   A. the knowledge of and familiarity with work operations
   B. the means of control of personnel, material, or job costs
   C. the means for communicating with other workers
   D. a useful method for making filing procedures easier

   5.___

6. The one of the following which is the MOST important factor in determining the number of employees you can effectively supervise is the

   A. type of work to be performed
   B. priority of the work to be performed
   C. salary level of the workers
   D. ratio of permanent employees to temporary employees

6._____

7. Of the following, you will be MOST productive in carrying out your supervisory responsibilities if you

   A. are capable of doing the same work as your mechanics
   B. meet with your mechanics frequently
   C. are very friendly with your mechanics
   D. get work done through your mechanics

7._____

8. You have been asked to prepare the annual budget for your maintenance shop.
The one of the following which is the FIRST step you should take in preparing this budget is to determine the

   A. amount of maintenance work which is scheduled for the shop
   B. time it takes for a specific unit of work to be completed
   C. current workload of each employee in the shop
   D. policies and procedures of the shop's operations

8._____

9. When determining the amount of work you expect a group of mechanics to perform in a given time, the BEST procedure for you to follow should be to

   A. aim for a higher level of production than that of the most productive worker
   B. stay at the present production level
   C. set general instead of specific goals
   D. let workers participate in the determination whenever possible

9._____

10. You have been asked to set next year's performance goals concerning the ratio of jobs completed on schedule to total jobs worked. A review of last year's record shows that the workers completed their jobs on schedule 85% of the time, with the best ones showing an on-time ratio of 92% and the poorest ones showing an on-time ratio of 65%.
Using these facts in line with generally accepted goal-setting practices, you should set a performance ratio for the next year on the basis of _____ average with a _____ minimum acceptable for any employee.

   A. 85%; 65%   B. 85%; 70%   C. 90%; 65%   D. 90%; 70%

10._____

11. It is important for you to be able to identify the critical parts of a large project such as the remodeling of your maintenance shop.
The one of the following which is the BEST reason why this is important is that it may

   A. help you to set up good communications between you and your workers
   B. give you a better understanding of the purpose of the project
   C. give you control over the time and cost involved in the project
   D. help you to determine who are your most productive workers

11._____

12. When doing work planning for your shop, the factor that you should normally consider LAST among the following is knowing your

    A. major objectives
    B. record keeping system
    C. minor objectives
    D. priorities

13. You have the responsibility for ordering all materials for your maintenance shop. A listing of materials needed for the operations of your shop is long overdue. You realize that you are unable to find time to take care of the inventory personally because of a high priority project you have been working on which has been taking all of your time. You do not know when you will be finished with the project.
    The BEST of the following courses of action to take in handling this inventory matter is to

    A. request that you be taken off the project immediately so that you may take care of the inventory
    B. complete your high priority project and then do the inventory yourself
    C. volunteer to work overtime so that you may complete the inventory while continuing with the project
    D. assign the inventory work to a competent subordinate

14. You have the authority and responsibility for seeing that proper records are kept in your shop. Assume that you decide to delegate to a records clerk the responsibility for collecting the time sheets and the authority to make changes on the time sheets to correct the information when necessary.
    Of the following, which one is the BEST argument that can be made regarding your decision?

    A. *Unacceptable*; because you can delegate only your responsibility but none of your authority to the records clerk
    B. *Acceptable*; because you can delegate some of your authority and some of your responsibility to the records clerk
    C. *Unacceptable;* because you can delegate only your authority but none of your responsibility to the records clerk
    D. *Acceptable;* because you can delegate all your responsibility and all your authority to the records clerk

15. You will LEAST likely be able to do an effective job of controlling operating costs if you

    A. eliminate idle time
    B. reduce absenteeism
    C. raise your budget
    D. combine work operations

16. Of the following actions, the one which is LEAST likely to help in carrying out your responsibilities of looking after the interests of your workers is to

    A. crack down on your workers when necessary
    B. let your workers know that you support company policy
    C. prevent the transfers of your workers
    D. back up your workers in a controversy

17. The term *accountability*, as used in management of supervision, means MOST NEARLY

    A. responsibility for results
    B. record keeping
    C. bookkeeping systems
    D. inventory control

18. Assume that you have been unable to convince an employee of the seriousness of his poor attendance record by talking to him.
    The one of the following which is the BEST course of action for you to take is to

    A. keep talking to the employee
    B. recommend that a written warning be given
    C. consider transferring the employee to another work location
    D. recommend that the employee be fired

19. When delegating work to a subordinate foreman, you should NOT

    A. delegate the right to make any decisions
    B. be interested in the results of the work, but in the method of doing the work
    C. delegate any work that you can do better than your subordinate
    D. give up your final responsibility for the work

20. Of the following statements, the BEST reason why proper scheduling of maintenance work is important is that it

    A. eliminates the need for individual job work orders
    B. classifies job skills in accordance with performance
    C. minimizes lost time in performing any maintenance job
    D. determines needed repairs in various locations

21. Of the following factors, the one which is of LEAST importance in determining the number of subordinates that an individual should be assigned to supervise is the

    A. nature of the work being supervised
    B. qualifications of the individual as a supervisor
    C. capabilities of the subordinates
    D. lines of promotion for the subordinates

22. Suppose that a large number of semi-literate residents of this city have been requesting the assistance of your department. You are asked to prepare a form which these applicants will be required to fill out before their requests will be considered.
    In view of these facts, the one of the following factors to which you should give the GREATEST amount of consideration in preparing this form is the

    A. size of the form
    B. sequence of the information asked for on the form
    C. level of difficulty of the language used in the form
    D. number of times which the form will have to be reviewed

23. A budget is a plan whereby a goal is set for future operations. It affords a medium for comparing actual expenditures with planned expenditures.
    The one of the following which is the MOST accurate statement on the basis of this statement is that

    A. the budget serves as an accurate measure of past as well as future expenditures
    B. the budget presents an estimate of expenditures to be made in the future
    C. budget estimates should be based upon past budget requirements
    D. planned expenditures usually fall short of actual expenditures

24. A foreman who is familiar with modern management principles should know that the one of the following requirements of an administrator which is LEAST important is his ability to

    A. coordinate work
    B. plan, organize, and direct the work under his control
    C. cooperate with others
    D. perform the duties of the employees under his jurisdiction

25. The one of the following which should be considered the LEAST important objective of the service rating system is to

    A. rate the employees on the basis of their potential abilities
    B. establish a basis for assigning employees to special types of work
    C. provide a means of recognizing superior work performance
    D. reveal the need for training as well as the effectiveness of a training program

KEY (CORRECT ANSWERS)

1.	A	11.	C
2.	A	12.	B
3.	B	13.	D
4.	C	14.	B
5.	B	15.	C
6.	A	16.	C
7.	D	17.	A
8.	A	18.	B
9.	D	19.	D
10.	D	20.	C

21. D
22. C
23. B
24. D
25. A

EXAMINATION SECTION
TEST 1

DIRECTIONS: Each question or incomplete statement is followed by several suggested answers or completions. Select the one that BEST answers the question or completes the statement. *PRINT THE LETTER OF THE CORRECT ANSWER IN THE SPACE AT THE RIGHT.*

1. Assume that the ticket agent at the bathhouse cannot dispense tickets from his machine because of a mechanical failure.
   You should authorize the ticket agent to

   A. sell tickets by hand from the bundle only
   B. stop selling tickets and await the installation of a stand-by machine
   C. collect cash from the patrons and have them escorted through the bathhouse entrance gate
   D. let the patrons deposit admission fees in a box at the bathhouse entrance gate

   1.____

2. If an operator of a four-wheel drive beach buggy leaves the sand portion of a beach and neglects to disengage his forward gears when he starts to drive over area streets to the dump or drop area, he will

   A. cause his transmission to lose linkage
   B. excessively wear his emergency brake
   C. jam up his front differential
   D. seriously damage the springs of the vehicle

   2.____

3. Inventories and replacement of material, supplies, and equipment required for pre-season preparation of beaches is normally scheduled to begin immediately after

   A. April 1st   B. Memorial Day
   C. Labor Day   D. New Year's Day

   3.____

4. On an Emerson Resuscitator, the cylinder is considered full when the cylinder volume indicator shows AT LEAST _____ lbs. pressure per square inch or more.

   A. 900   B. 1300   C. 1800   D. 2800

   4.____

5. The term *deadman,* when used in training courses for lifeguards assigned to oceanfront beaches, refers to

   A. a rope splicing tool
   B. beach cradles
   C. upland anchorage
   D. a fixed warning sign on a stone jetty

   5.____

6. The appropriate arm signal for a lifeguard to give from a standing position on his tower to call for delivery of a resuscitator is:

   A. Pump one arm up and down from an overhead position
   B. Rotary motion in front of chest
   C. Arms extended up -- straight overhead
   D. Arms clasped overhead

   6.____

7. The standard technique for executing the back pressure - arm lift method of artificial respiration requires the operator to adhere to a cycle consisting of a prescribed series of motions.
   This cycle should be repeated about _____ times per minute.

   A. two   B. four   C. six   D. twelve

8. Assume that an elderly swimmer has collapsed while swimming. His friend, who is with him, states that the victim has a long history of heart failure. The victim is brought to the first aid station showing signs of shock and labored breathing.
   You should take which one of the following actions?

   A. Apply an oxygen mask tightly to the victim's face
   B. Using the resuscitator, turn on the inhalator valve and apply the face mask
   C. Get him dressed and send him to a hospital with his friend
   D. Wrap him in blankets to keep warm and give him a hot beverage

9. The symptoms of heat prostration MOST usually are:

   A. Face pale, pulse weak; perspiration profuse on forehead, face, and hands; faintness and nausea
   B. Face red, hot, and dry; pulse strong and fast, high fever; perhaps nausea
   C. Face purplish; pulse erratic; feet and hands cold
   D. Face pale; respiration rate down to six; patient violent

10. Of the following, the BEST method for controlling algae growth in outdoor swimming pools is to

    A. treat with heavy dosages of chlorine
    B. raise the pH with additional amounts of calcium carbonate
    C. apply standard rates of copper sulphate
    D. lower the pool level and add fresh water from the main

11. To improve the capabilities of swimming pool filters, a jelly-like substance called a *flock* must be deposited on the surface of the filter bed.
    The flock is formed by adding which of the following two chemicals to the water in the treatment tank?

    A. Anhydrous ammonia and sodium dichromate
    B. Aluminum sulphate and sodium carbonate
    C. Orthotolidine and copper sulphate
    D. Iodides and calcium chloride

12. Pool water returning from the center drain of an outdoor swimming pool is called the

    A. confluent   B. effluent   C. influent   D. affluent

13. Backwashing in a conventional water treatment plant is USUALLY performed by the plant operator when the loss of head reaches _____ pounds per square inch.

    A. 3 1/2-4   B. 5 1/2-7   C. 8-10   D. 11-12

14. Most outdoor swimming pool operations have large heating boilers. These boilers have water columns with look-through water gauges, showing the water level in the boiler. The manual on maintenance and operation of heating plants and auxiliary equipment specifies that, while the boiler is in operation, the water column and gauge glass should be blown down

    A. daily B. weekly C. bi-weekly D. monthly

    14.____

15. Conventional gun-type oil burners used at park facilities are required to utilize as fuel

    A. #2 oil
    B. #4 oil
    C. #6 oil
    D. a kerosene mixture

    15.____

16. Chlorine residual in municipally operated pools as required by the department of health shall be kept at NOT LESS THAN _____ ppm.

    A. 0.01 B. 0.25 C. 0.45 D. 1.0

    16.____

17. Which of the following should be used to test the pH range (alkaline range) of swimming pool water?

    A. Ultraviolet light
    B. Iodides
    C. Orthotolodine
    D. Bromthymol blue

    17.____

18. The filtration rate per square foot for a conventional filter is _____ gallons per square foot.

    A. 8 B. 6 C. 5 D. 3

    18.____

19. Chlorine gas in steel cylinders is used as a sterilant in most outdoor swimming pools. If chlorine gas leaks occur from faulty connections, valve packings, etc., the STANDARD procedure for locating the leaks promptly is to use

    A. a lighted sulphur taper
    B. a soapy mixture
    C. acetone, applied with a camel hair brush
    D. concentrated ammonia

    19.____

20. The MOST desirable time to apply lime to fairways on a golf course that is high in the acid range is

    A. during the rainy season
    B. after a long, dry spell
    C. in the fall or spring
    D. in late January

    20.____

21. A bag of commercial fertilizer with a 10-6-4 classification on the printed face of the bag contains which of the following combination of chemicals by weight?

    A. 10% phosphoric acid, 6% nitrogen, and 4% potash
    B. 10% potash, 6% phosphoric acid, and 4% nitrogen
    C. 10% nitrogen, 6% phosphoric acid, and 4% potash
    D. 10% potash, 6% nitrogen, and 4% phosphoric acid

    21.____

22. The turf on a tee with 15,000 square feet is badly worn because of traffic density and must be completely rehabilitated. You have completed the step requiring the application of a soil sterilant, and you are ready to apply nitrogen to the soil at a rate of two pounds of available nitrogen per thousand square feet.
How many 100 pound bags of 10-6-4 fertilizer must be applied to adequately supply the nitrogen requirements?

    A. 10   B. 8   C. 5   D. 3

23. According to regulations relating to lawn-making, which of the following pH ratings of fertilizer is desirable?

    A. 4.5 to 5.0   B. 5.5 to 6.0
    C. 6.5 to 7.0   D. 7.5 to 8.0

24. To facilitate photosynthesis for normal growth, grass should be mowed often enough so that clippings are

    A. equal to mowing height
    B. shorter than mowing height
    C. longer than mowing height
    D. two inches long

25. Of the following, the MOST suitable grass seed mixture for a play field is one containing Kentucky bluegrass and

    A. colonial bent   B. Bermuda grass
    C. zoysia   D. creeping red fescue

26. Red fescue is USUALLY added to a seed mixture because of its

    A. drought resistance   B. fast germination
    C. slow germination   D. coarse texture

27. The four basic procedures generally considered as constituting the minimum maintenance for turf are: (1) selection of adapted grasses; (2) fertilization; (3) watering; and (4)

    A. aerification   B. mowing
    C. plugging   D. rolling

28. The BEST method for improving the soil structure of a heavily compacted playfield is to apply organic top-dressing first and then proceed with

    A. pesticide application   B. mowing and watering
    C. fertilization   D. aerification

29. A fairway should be maintained so that its width averages _____ to _____ feet.

    A. 60; 110   B. 120; 210   C. 220; 260   D. 270; 310

30. A good supplemental program to aid the grass that is already growing and to establish new grass in the thin, worn-out areas of an athletic field is

    A. overseeding   B. rolling
    C. plugging   D. watering

KEY (CORRECT ANSWERS)

1.	A	11.	B	21.	C
2.	C	12.	B	22.	D
3.	C	13.	B	23.	C
4.	C	14.	A	24.	B
5.	C	15.	A	25.	D
6.	C	16.	D	26.	A
7.	D	17.	D	27.	B
8.	B	18.	D	28.	D
9.	A	19.	D	29.	B
10.	C	20.	C	30.	A

TEST 2

DIRECTIONS: Each question or incomplete statement is followed by several suggested answers or completions. Select the one that BEST answers the question or completes the statement. *PRINT THE LETTER OF THE CORRECT ANSWER IN THE SPACE AT THE RIGHT.*

1. Traps are customarily surfaced with a layer of sand about _____ inches deep. 1.___
   A. 6 B. 12 C. 18 D. 24

2. A GOOD medium sandy loam for a putting green should contain _____ organic content. 2.___
   A. 5-10% B. 10-15% C. 20-30% D. 30-50%

3. In the maintenance of a putting green, the LEAST necessary piece of equipment is 3.___
   A. putting green mower
   B. power sprayer
   C. aerator
   D. fertilizer spreader

4. The BEST way to maintain a green so that it holds a pitched ball is by 4.___
   A. overwatering
   B. good soil structure
   C. underwatering
   D. high mowing

5. The surface soil on a green should be a medium sandy loam placed _____ to _____ inches deep. 5.___
   A. 2; 4 B. 4; 6 C. 8; 10 D. 12; 18

6. The BEST turf fertilizers today contain about 6.___
   A. 85% slow-release phosphorus
   B. 16% fast-release nitrogen
   C. 50% slow-release nitrogen
   D. 20% phosphorus

7. Since golf course grasses are heavy users of phosphorus, potassium, magnesium, and calcium, the BEST pH range for turf, where maximum quantities of these chemicals are available, is 7.___
   A. 4.2 to 4.8
   B. 5.0 to 5.8
   C. 6.0 to 7.0
   D. 7.2 to 8.2

8. Damage on golf greens and other turf areas caused by the *Fusarium nivale* fungus (snow mold) can BEST be prevented or adequately checked by treatment with 8.___
   A. ammonium methyl arsenates
   B. aluminum sulphate
   C. hydrated lime
   D. cadminates

9. To prevent snow mold, treatment should GENERALLY start 9.___
   A. in early spring
   B. after a heavy rain
   C. in late winter
   D. after a heavy snow

10. Chlordane is used in turf management to

   A. eradicate goose grass
   B. control brown patch
   C. grub-proof soil
   D. stimulate root growth

11. Artificial rinks have refrigerants to cool the brine which is constantly circulated through the wrought-iron pipes imbedded in the floor of the rink.
   The brine can be chilled to below zero degrees Fahrenheit because it contains a chemical salt known as

   A. sodium chloride
   B. calcium chloride
   C. calcium carbonate
   D. ammonium chloride

12. The MINIMUM ice thickness generally considered safe for ice skating on a lake or pond whose depth does not exceed 3 feet is _____ inches.

   A. 2
   B. 3
   C. 5
   D. 6

13. In the operation of an ice skating rink, prior to starting the process of ice building, the slab surface should be painted with _____ paint.

   A. white water
   B. white epoxy
   C. blue water
   D. blue epoxy

14. Crowd control in an ice skating rink includes all phases of the patrons' activities from admissions line-up to the time the patrons leave the rink.
   According to regulations, during special sessions, guards should

   A. skate in a clockwise direction
   B. skate in a counterclockwise direction
   C. be positioned on the ice near the entrances
   D. be positioned off the ice near the entrances

15. When a rink slab has been chilled below freezing temperature, ice can be built to the desired thickness by spraying a fine layer of water onto the slab with a

   A. Toro sprayer
   B. Skinner sprinkler
   C. Rainboni
   D. Zamboni

16. The following is a description of the cooling system of a skating rink: The refrigerant (ammonia or freon) absorbs the heat from the circulating brine which, in turn, lowers the temperature of the skating slab; when the brine is returned to the chiller after leaving the rink floor with absorbed heat, the compressor pumps the refrigerant gases to the condenser.
   The condenser does which of the following?
   It

   A. cools the refrigerant gas to a liquid and returns it to the chiller
   B. heats up the refrigerant gas
   C. transforms the gas into ice crystals
   D. cools the circulating water within the condenser

17. At indoor rinks where atmospheric temperatures remain stable and are not affected by outdoor weather conditions, brine should be circulated at a temperature of APPROXIMATELY _____ degrees Fahrenheit.

   A. 7
   B. 10
   C. 15
   D. 25

18. Conditioning ice surfaces on outdoor rinks in early fall or late spring is BEST accomplished

    A. after each session
    B. after the sun sets
    C. at 8 A.M.
    D. at 12 noon

19. The standard of thickness for safe skating on lakes and ponds with water depths over three feet is _____ inches.

    A. two
    B. three
    C. five
    D. seven

20. Assume that a heavy snowstorm has reached the area at the start of the evening session of outdoor rink operations. The one of the following actions that should be taken is to

    A. send all the skaters home, telling them the rink is closed
    B. let them skate until the snow is too deep to move
    C. cone off one-half of the rink at a time for snow removal operations
    D. give snow shovels to as many skaters as possible and put them to work clearing the rink

21. Of the following trees, the one which is NOT recommended for street tree planting is

    A. London plane
    B. Gingko
    C. Yellow Pine
    D. Pin Oak

22. Before useful measures can be applied to control a tree disease epidemic in a park, it is FIRST necessary to

    A. obtain an appropriation for spraying
    B. have a correct diagnosis made of the disease
    C. make an inventory of the diseased trees
    D. wait until winter when the trees are dormant

23. Of the following trees, the one which is generally MOST often recommended for sandy soils is

    A. American elm
    B. Japanese maple
    C. Chinese poplar
    D. Japanese black pine

24. About 75 percent of all tree diseases, including all mildews, rusts, anthracnoses, and sooty molds, are caused by

    A. fungi
    B. viruses
    C. nematodes
    D. bacteria

25. Tree crews should be instructed to ALWAYS

    A. trim the leader of a tree to improve its vitality
    B. prune trees by removing at least 50% of the crowns
    C. remove all injured and diseased wood
    D. fertilize a tree before pruning it

26. Three techniques that you can use to evaluate maintenance activities and determine whether they can be done better are work simplification, work measurement, and

   A. establishment of work performance standards
   B. use of labor saving devices
   C. increased supervision
   D. computerization

27. Staffing is BEST indicated by which of the following activities?

   A. Selection and training of personnel and maintaining favorable conditions of work
   B. Structuring an organization for unity of command, span of control, and lines of authority
   C. Writing task lists for the different titles working at a facility
   D. Working out in broad outline the things that need to be done and the methods for doing them to accomplish the mission of the agency

28. Generally, the MOST practical way to ascertain most readily the number of man-hours it takes to do a job is by

   A. referring to a management analysis handbook
   B. making a detailed analysis of the job
   C. asking the operator performing the job
   D. reviewing job specifications

29. Any violation of the rules or regulations for the government and protection of public parks and property shall be punishable by NOT MORE THAN _____ imprisonment or by a fine of not more than _____ dollars, or by both.

   A. thirty days'; fifty
   B. sixty days'; one hundred
   C. ninety days'; two hundred fifty
   D. one year's; five hundred

30. One workman can hand-rake leaves at the rate of approximately 1,000 square feet in 20 minutes.
   How many men would you assign to a crew to hand rake a grove of trees covering 40,000 square feet in order to accomplish the job within three hours?

   A. 3   B. 30   C. 50   D. 5

KEY (CORRECT ANSWERS)

1.	A	11.	B	21.	C
2.	C	12.	B	22.	B
3.	B	13.	A	23.	D
4.	B	14.	D	24.	A
5.	C	15.	D	25.	C
6.	C	16.	A	26.	A
7.	C	17.	C	27.	A
8.	D	18.	A	28.	C
9.	A	19.	C	29.	A
10.	C	20.	C	30.	D

PREPARING WRITTEN MATERIAL
EXAMINATION SECTION
TEST 1

DIRECTIONS: Each of the following sentences may be classified under one of the following four categories:
A. *Faulty* because of incorrect grammar or usage
B. *Faulty* because of incorrect punctuation or spelling
C. *Faulty* because of incorrect capitalization
D. *Correct*

Examine each sentence carefully. Then, in the correspondingly numbered space on the right, print the capital letter preceding the option which is the best of the four suggested above.

(All incorrect sentences contain but one type of error. Consider a sentence correct if it contains none of the types of errors mentioned, even though there may be other correct ways of expressing the same thought.

1. They gave the poor man some food when he approached. 1.____
2. I regret the loss caused by the error. 2.____
3. The students have a new teacher for shop mantenance. 3.____
4. They sweared to bring out all the facts. 4.____
5. He decided to open a branch store on 33rd street. 5.____
6. His speed is equal and more than that of a racehorse. 6.____
7. He felt very warm on that Summer day. 7.____
8. He was assisted by his friend, who lives in the next house. 8.____
9. The climate of New York is colder than California. 9.____
10. I shall wait for you on the corner. 10.____
11. Did we see the boy whose the leader? 11.____
12. Being a modest person, John seldom takes about his invention. 12.____
13. The gang is called the smith street boys. 13.____
14. He seen the man break into the store. 14.____

2 (#1)

15. We expected to lay still there for quite a while. 15.____
16. He is considered to be the Leader of his organization. 16.____
17. Although He received an invitation, He won't go. 17.____
18. The letter must be here some place. 18.____
19. I thought it to be he. 19.____
20. We expect to remain here for a long time. 20.____
21. The committee was agreed. 21.____
22. Two-thirds of the building are finished. 22.____
23. The water was froze. 23.____
24. Everyone of the salesmen must supply their own car. 24.____
25. Who is the author of Gone With the Wind? 25.____
26. He marched on and declaring that he would never surrender. 26.____
27. Who shall I say called? 27.____
28. Everyone has left but they. 28.____
29. Who did we give the order to? 29.____
30. Send your order in immediately. 30.____
31. I believe I paid the Bill. 31.____
32. I have not met but one person. 32.____
33. Why aren't Tom, and Fred, going to the dance? 33.____
34. What reason is there for him not going? 34.____
35. The seige of Malta was a tremendous event. 35.____
36. I was there yesterday I assure you. 36.____
37. Your ukulele is better than mine. 37.____
38. No one was there only Mary. 38.____

3 (#1)

39. The Capital city of Vermont is Montpelier. 39._____

40. Reggie Jackson may hit the largest amount of home runs this season. 40._____

KEY (CORRECT ANSWERS)

1.	B	11.	B	21.	D	31.	C
2.	D	12.	D	22.	A	32.	A
3.	B	13.	C	23.	A	33.	B
4.	A	14.	A	24.	A	34.	A
5.	C	15.	A	25.	B	35.	B
6.	A	16.	C	26.	A	36.	B
7.	C	17.	C	27.	D	37.	B
8.	D	18.	A	28.	D	38.	A
9.	A	19.	A	29.	A	39.	C
10.	D	20.	D	30.	D	40.	A

TEST 2

Questions 1-3.

DIRECTIONS: Questions 1 through 3 each consist of four sentences. Choose the one sentence in each set of four that would be BEST for a formal letter or report. Consider grammar and appropriate usage.

1. A. Most all the work he completed before he become ill.
    B. He completed most of the work before becoming ill.
    C. Prior to him becoming ill his work was mostly completed.
    D. Before he became will most of the work he had completed.

    1.____

2. A. Being that the report lacked a clearly worded recommendation, it did not matter that it contained enough information.
    B. There was enough information in the report, although it, including the recommendation, were not clearly worded.
    C. Although the report contained enough information, it did not have a clearly worded recommendation.
    D. Though the report did not have a recommendation that was clearly worded, and the information therein contained was enough.

    2.____

3. A. Having already overlooked the important mistakes, the ones which she found were not as important toward the end of the letter.
    B. Toward the end of the letter she had already overlooked the important mistakes, so that which she had found were not important.
    C. The mistakes which she had already overlooked were not as important as those which near the end of letter she had found.
    D. The mistakes which she found near the end of the letter were not so important as those which she had already overlooked.

    3.____

Questions 4-5.

DIRECTIONS: Select the correct answer.

4. The unit has exceeded _____ goals and the employees are satisfied with _____ accomplishments.
    A. their; it's   B. it's, it's   C. is, there   D. its, their

    4.____

5. Research indicates that employees who _____ no opportunity for close social relationships often find their work unsatisfying, and this _____ of satisfaction often reflects itself in low production.
    A. have, lack   B. have, excess   C. has, lack   D. has, excess

    5.____

2 (#2)

KEY (CORRECT ANSWERS)

1. B
2. C
3. D
4. D
5. A

TEST 3

DIRECTIONS: Select the choice which BEST expresses the thought and which contains NO errors in grammar or sentence construction.

1. A. She, hearing a signal, the source lamp flashed.
   B. While hearing a signal, the source lamp flashed
   C. In hearing a signal, the source lamp flashed.
   D. As she heard a signal, the source lamp flashed.

   1.____

2. A. Every one of the time records have been initialed in the designated spaces.
   B. All of the time records has been initialed in the designated spaces.
   C. Which one of the time records was initialed in the designated spaces.
   D. The time records all been initialed in the designated spaces.

   2.____

3. A. If there is no one else to answer the phone, you will have to answer it.
   B. You will have to answer it yourself if no one else answers the phone.
   C. If no one else is not around to pick up the phone, you have to do it.
   D. You will have to answer the phone when nobodys here to do it.

   3.____

4. A. Dr. Byrnes not in his office. What could I do for you?
   B. Dr. Byrnes is not in his office. Is there something I can do for you?
   C. Since Dr. Byrnes is not in his office, might there be something I may do for you?
   D. Is there any ways I can assist you since Dr. Brynes is not in his office?

   4.____

5. A. She do not understand how the new console works.
   B. The way the new console works, she doesn't understand.
   C. She doesn't understand how the new console works.
   D. The new console works, so that she doesn't understand.

   5.____

KEY (CORRECT ANSWERS)

1. D
2. C
3. A
4. B
5. C

TEST 4

DIRECTIONS: The following questions each consist of a sentence which may or may not be an example of good English usage.

Consider grammar, punctuation, spelling, capitalization, awkwardness, etc.

Examine each sentence and then choose the correct statement about it from the four choices below. If the English usage in the sentence given is better than any of the changes suggested in options B, C, or D, choose option A. (Do not choose an option that will change the meaning of the sentence.)

1. The typist used an extention cord in order to connect her typewriter to the outlet nearest to her desk.
    A. This is an example of acceptable writing.
    B. A period should be placed after the word "cord" and the word "in" should have a capital "I."
    C. A comma should be placed after the word "typewriter."
    D. The word "extention" should be spelled "extension."

2. He would have went to the conference if he had received an invitation.
    A. This is an example of acceptable writing.
    B. The word "went" should be replaced by the word "gone."
    C. The word "had" should be replaced by "would have."
    D. The word "conference" should be spelled "conference."

3. In order to make the report neater, he spent many hours rewriting it.
    A. This is an example of acceptable writing.
    B. The word "more" should be inserted before the word "neater."
    C. There should be a colon after the word "neater."
    D. The word "spent" should be changed to "have spent."

4. His supervisor told him that he should of read the memorandum more carefully.
    A. This is an example of acceptable writing.
    B. The word "memorandum" should be spelled "memorandom."
    C. The word "of" should be replaced by the word "have."
    D. The word "carefully" should be replaced by the word "have."

5. It was decided that two separate reports should be written.
    A. This is an example of acceptable writing.
    B. A comma should be inserted after the word "decided."
    C. The word "be" should be replaced by the word "been."
    D. A colon should be inserted after the word "that."

6. She don't seem to understand that the work must be done as soon as possible.
    A. This is an example of acceptable writing.
    B. The word "doesn't" should replace the word "don't."
    C. The word "why" should replace the word "that."
    D. The word "as" before the word "soon" should be eliminated.

KEY (CORRECT ANSWERS)

1. D
2. B
3. A
4. C
5. A
6. B

PREPARING WRITTEN MATERIAL
EXAMINATION SECTION
TEST 1

DIRECTIONS: Each of Questions 1 through 5 consists of a sentence which may or may not be an example of good formal English usage. Examine each sentence, considering grammar, punctuation, spelling, capitalization, and awkwardness. Then choose the correct statement about it from the four options below it. If the English usage in the sentence given is better than any of the changes suggested in options B, C, or D, pick option A. (Do not pick an option that will change the meaning of the sentence.) *PRINT THE LETTER OF THE CORRECT ANSWER IN THE SPACE AT THE RIGHT.*

1. I don't know who could possibly of broken it.
   A. This is an example of good formal English usage.
   B. The word "who" should be replaced by the word "whom."
   C. The word "of" should be replaced by the word "have."
   D. The word "broken" should be replaced by the word "broke."

2. Telephoning is easier than to write.
   A. This is an example of good formal English usage.
   B. The word "telephoning" should be spelled "telephoneing."
   C. The word "than" should be replaced by the word "then."
   D. The words "to write" should be replaced by the word "writing."

3. The two operators who have been assigned to these consoles are on vacation.
   A. This is an example of good formal English usage.
   B. A comma should be placed after the word "operators."
   C. The word "who" should be replaced by the word "whom."
   D. The word "are" should be replaced by the word "is."

4. You were suppose to teach me how to operate a plugboard.
   A. This is an example of good formal English usage.
   B. The word "were" should be replaced by the word "was."
   C. The word "suppose" should be replaced by the word "supposed."
   D. The word "teach" should be replaced by the word "learn."

5. If you had taken my advice; you would have spoken with him.
   A. This is an example of good formal English usage.
   B. The word "advice" should be spelled "advise."
   C. The words "had taken" should be replaced by the word "take."
   D. The semicolon should be changed to a comma.

2 (#1)

KEY (CORRECT ANSWERS)

1. C
2. D
3. A
4. C
5. D

TEST 2

DIRECTIONS: Select the correct answer. *PRINT THE LETTER OF THE CORRECT ANSWER IN THE SPACE AT THE RIGHT.*

1. The one of the following sentences which is MOST acceptable from the viewpoint of correct grammatical usage is:
   A. I do not know which action will have worser results.
   B. He should of known better.
   C. Both the officer on the scene, and his immediate supervisor, is charged with the responsibility.
   D. An officer must have initiative because his supervisor will not always be available to answer questions.

   1.____

2. The one of the following sentences which is MOST acceptable from the viewpoint of correct grammatical usage is:
   A. Of all the officers available, the better one for the job will be picked.
   B. Strict orders were given to all the officers, except he.
   C. Study of the law will enable you to perform your duties more efficiently.
   D. It seems to me that you was wrong in failing to search the two men.

   2.____

3. The one of the following sentences which does NOT contain a misspelled word is:
   A. The duties you will perform are similar to the duties of a patrolman.
   B. Officers must be constantly alert to sieze the initiative.
   C. Officers in this organization are not entitled to special privileges.
   D. Any changes in procedure will be announced publically.

   3.____

4. The one of the following sentences which does NOT contain a misspelled word is:
   A. It will be to your advantage to keep your firearm in good working condition.
   B. There are approximately fourty men on sick leave.
   C. Your first duty will be to pursuade the person to obey the law.
   D. Fires often begin in flameable material kept in lockers.

   4.____

5. The one of the following sentences which does NOT contain a misspelled word is:
   A. Offices are not required to perform technical maintainance.
   B. He violated the regulations on two occasions.
   C. Every employee will be held responable for errors.
   D. This was his nineth absence in a year.

   5.____

KEY (CORRECT ANSWERS)

1. D
2. C
3. C
4. A
5. B

TEST 3

DIRECTIONS: Select the correct answer. *PRINT THE LETTER OF THE CORRECT ANSWER IN THE SPACE AT THE RIGHT.*

1. You are answering a letter that was written on the letterhead of the ABC Company and signed by James H. Wood, Treasurer.
   What is usually considered to be the correct salutation to use in your reply?
   A. Dear ABC Company:
   B. Dear Sirs:
   C. Dear Mr. Wood:
   D. Dear Mr. Treasurer:

   1._____

2. Assume that one of your duties is to handle routine letters of inquiry from the public.
   The one of the following which is usually considered to be MOST desirable in replying to such a letter is a
   A. detailed answer handwritten on the original letter of inquiry
   B. phone call, since you can cover details more easily over the phone than in a letter
   C. short letter giving the specific information requested
   D. long letter discussing all possible aspects of the question raised

   2._____

3. The CHIEF reason for dividing a letter into paragraphs is to
   A. make the message clear to the reader by starting a new paragraph for each new topic
   B. make a short letter occupy as much of the page as possible
   C. keep the reader's attention by providing a pause from time to time
   D. make the letter look neat and businesslike

   3._____

4. Your superior has asked you to send an e-mail from your agency to a government agency in another city. He has written out the message and has indicated the name of the government agency.
   When you dictate the message to your secretary, which of the following items that your superior has NOT mentioned must you be sure to include?
   A. Today's date
   B. The full address of the government agency
   C. A polite opening such as "Dear Sirs"
   D. A final sentence such as "We would appreciate hearing from your agency in reply as soon as is convenient for you"

   4._____

5. The one of the following sentences which is grammatically preferable to the others is:
   A. Our engineers will go over your blueprints so that you may have no problems in construction.
   B. For a long time he had been arguing that we, not he, are to blame for the confusion.
   C. I worked on this automobile for two hours and still cannot find out what is wrong with it.
   D. Accustomed to all kinds of hardships, fatigue seldom bothers veteran policemen.

   5._____

KEY (CORRECT ANSWERS)

1. C
2. C
3. A
4. B
5. A

TEST 4

DIRECTIONS: Select the correct answer. *PRINT THE LETTER OF THE CORRECT ANSWER IN THE SPACE AT THE RIGHT.*

1. Suppose that an applicant for a job as snow laborer presents a letter from a former employer stating: "John Smith has a pleasing manner and never got into an argument with his fellow employees. He was never late or absent." This letter
    A. indicates that with some training Smith will make a good snow gang boss
    B. presents no definite evidence of Smith's ability to do snow work
    C. proves definitely that Smith has never done any snow work before
    D. proves definitely that Smith will do better than average work as a snow laborer

    1.____

2. Suppose you must write a letter to a local organization in your section refusing a request in connection with collection of their refuse.
   You should start the letter by
    A. explaining in detail the consideration you gave the request
    B. praising the organization for its service to the community
    C. quoting the regulation which forbids granting the request
    D. stating your regret that the request cannot be granted

    2.____

3. Suppose a citizen writes in for information as to whether or not he may sweep refuse into the gutter. A Sanitation officer answers as follows:
   Dear Sir:
     No person is permitted to litter, sweep, throw or cast, or direct, suffer or permit any person under his control to litter, sweep, throw or cast any ashes, garbage, paper, dust, or other rubbish or refuse into any public street or place, vacant lot, air shaft, areaway, backyard or court.
                                     Very truly yours,
                                     John Doe
   This letter is *poorly* written CHIEFLY because
    A. the opening is not indented   B. the thought is not clear
    C. the tone is too formal and cold   D. there are too many commas used

    3.____

4. A section of a disciplinary report written by a Sanitation officer states: "It is requested that subject Sanitation man be advised that his future activities be directed towards reducing his recurrent tardiness else disciplinary action will be initiated which may result in summary discharge."
   This section of the report is *poorly* written MAINLY because
    A. at least one word is misspelled   B. it is not simply expressed
    C. more than one idea is expressed   D. the purpose is not stated

    4.____

5. A section of a disciplinary report written by an officer states: "He comes in late. He takes too much time for lunch. He is lazy. I recommend his services be dispensed with."
   This section of the report is *poorly* written MAINLY because
    A. it ends with a preposition   B. it is not well organized
    C. no supporting facts are stated   D. the sentences are too simple

    5.____

107

KEY (CORRECT ANSWERS)

1. B
2. D
3. C
4. B
5. C

PREPARING WRITTEN MATERIAL

PARAGRAPH REARRANGEMENT
COMMENTARY

The sentences that follow are in scrambled order. You are to rearrange them in proper order and indicate the letter choice containing the correct answer at the space at the right.

Each group of sentences in this section is actually a paragraph presented in scrambled order. Each sentence in the group has a place in that paragraph; no sentence is to be left out. You are to read each group of sentences and decide upon the best order in which to put the sentences so as to form a well-organized paragraph.

The questions in this section measure the ability to solve a problem when all the facts relevant to its solution are not given.

More specifically, certain positions of responsibility and authority require the employee to discover connection between events sometimes, apparently, unrelated. In order to do this, the employee will find it necessary to correctly infer that unspecified events have probably occurred or are likely to occur. This ability becomes especially important when action must be taken on incomplete information.

Accordingly, these questions require competitors to choose among several suggested alternatives, each of which presents a different sequential arrangement of the events. Competitors must choose the MOST logical of the suggested sequences.

In order to do so, they may be required to draw on general knowledge to infer missing concepts or events that are essential to sequencing the given events. Competitors should be careful to infer only what is essential to the sequence. The plausibility of the wrong alternatives will always require the inclusion of unlikely events or of additional chains of events which are NOT essential to sequencing the given events.

It's very important to remember that you are looking for the best of the four possible choices, and that the best choice of all may not even be one of the answers you're given to choose from.

There is no one right way to solve these problems. Many people have found it helpful to first write out the order of the sentences, as they would have arranged them, on their scrap paper before looking at the possible answers. If their optimum answer is there, this can save them some time. If it isn't, this method can still give insight into solving the problem. Others find it most helpful to just go through each of the possible choices, contrasting each as they go along. You should use whatever method feels comfortable and works for you.

While most of these types of questions are not that difficult, we've added a higher percentage of the difficult type, just to give you more practice. Usually there are only one or two questions on this section that contain such subtle distinctions that you're unable to answer confidently. And you then may find yourself stuck deciding between two possible choices, neither of which you're sure about.

EXAMINATION SECTION
TEST 1

DIRECTIONS: Each group of sentences in this section is actually a paragraph presented in scrambled order. Each sentence in the group has a place in that paragraph; no sentence is to be left out. You are to read each group of sentences so as to form a well-organized paragraph. Before trying to answer the questions which follow each group of sentences, jot down the correct order of the sentences. Then answer each of the questions by printing the letter of the correct answer in the space at the right. Remember that you will receive credit only for answers marked.

P. It is unfounded because, while the weak resent the power of the strong, they also respect it.
Q. The hesitancy stems from a concern for public opinion in other countries.
R. The United States has ordinarily been ill at ease in using its military power in support of its interests.
S. The concern is largely unfounded.
T. The roots of American hesitancy are deeply imbedded in the American mind.

1. Which sentence did you put last?
   A. P   B. Q   C. R   D. S   E. T

2. Which sentence did you put after Sentence R?
   A. P
   B. Q
   C. S
   D. T
   E. None of the above. Sentence R is last.

3. Which sentence did you put before Sentence S?
   A. P
   B. Q

4. Which sentence did you put before Sentence R?
   A. P
   B. Q
   C. S
   D. T
   E. None of the above. Sentence R is last.

5. Which sentence did you put fourth?
   A. P   B. Q   C. R   D. S   E. T

KEY (CORRECT ANSWERS)

1. A
2. D
3. B
4. E
5. D

TEST 2

DIRECTIONS: Each group of sentences in this section is actually a paragraph presented in scrambled order. Each sentence in the group has a place in that paragraph; no sentence is to be left out. You are to read each group of sentences so as to form a well-organized paragraph. Before trying to answer the questions which follow each group of sentences, jot down the correct order of the sentences. Then answer each of the questions by printing the letter of the correct answer in the space at the right. Remember that you will receive credit only for answers marked.

P. Its lawlessness was virtually non-existent.
Q. The *Old West*, as portrayed in motion pictures, on television, and in books, is completely distorted.
R. It is obvious, therefore, that the *Old West* is falsely presented in mass media solely for commercial purposes.
S. Its heroes, too, were far from heroic.
T. Those who lived in the *Old West* in its final days, or talked to oldtimers, know the truth.

1. Which sentence did you put last?
   A. P   B. Q   C. R   D. S   E. T

2. Which sentence did you put after Sentence Q?
   A. P
   B. R
   C. S
   D. T
   E. None of the above. Sentence Q is last.

3. Which sentence did you put before Sentence S?
   A. P
   B. Q
   C. R
   D. T
   E. None of the above. Sentence S is first.

4. Which sentence did you put before Sentence Q?
   A. P
   B. R
   C. S
   D. T
   E. None of the above. Sentence Q is first.

5. Which sentence did you put after Sentence S? 5.____
    A. P
    B. Q
    C. R
    D. T
    E. None of the above. Sentence S is last.

KEY (CORRECT ANSWERS)

1. C
2. D
3. A
4. E
5. C

TEST 3

DIRECTIONS: Each group of sentences in this section is actually a paragraph presented in scrambled order. Each sentence in the group has a place in that paragraph; no sentence is to be left out. You are to read each group of sentences so as to form a well-organized paragraph. Before trying to answer the questions which follow each group of sentences, jot down the correct order of the sentences. Then answer each of the questions by printing the letter of the correct answer in the space at the right. Remember that you will receive credit only for answers marked.

P. One advertising executive became agitated recently when he suddenly realized that the floors of supermarkets were being unimaginatively used merely to walk on.
Q. Blank spaces, advertising men feel, cry out to be filled with merchandise-hustling messages.
R. He invented a slide projector which projects images on sheets of translucent plastic embedded in supermarket floors.
S. At once, he got to work to correct this unforgiveable oversight.
T. As nature abhors a vacuum, so do advertising men decry blank spaces.

1. Which sentence did you put last?
   A. P
   B. Q
   C. S
   D. T
   E. None of the above. Sentence R is last.

2. Which sentence did you put third?
   A. P   B. Q   C. R   D. S   E. T

3. Which sentence did you put before Sentence T?
   A. P
   B. Q
   C. R
   D. T
   E. None of the above. Sentence T is first.

4. Which sentence did you put after Sentence P?
   A. Q
   B. R
   C. S
   D. T
   E. None of the above. Sentence P is last.

5. Which sentence did you put before Sentence Q? 5.____
    A. P
    B. R
    C. S
    D. T
    E. None of the above. Sentence Q is last.

KEY (CORRECT ANSWERS)

1. E
2. A
3. E
4. C
5. D

TEST 4

DIRECTIONS: Each group of sentences in this section is actually a paragraph presented in scrambled order. Each sentence in the group has a place in that paragraph; no sentence is to be left out. You are to read each group of sentences so as to form a well-organized paragraph. Before trying to answer the questions which follow each group of sentences, jot down the correct order of the sentences. Then answer each of the questions by printing the letter of the correct answer in the space at the right. Remember that you will receive credit only for answers marked.

P. It is estimated that Americans smoked almost a trillion cigarettes in 2020, while they smoked only several hundred million cigars and pipefuls of tobacco.
Q. Originally, they were considered exclusively a *ladies'* smoke.
R. Only in this century did cigarettes become popular in the United States.
S. Far more Americans smoke cigarettes today than smoke cigars and pipes combined.
T. This was not always the case, however.

1. Which sentence did you put first?
   A. P   B. Q   C. R   D. S   E. T

2. Which sentence did you put after Sentence Q?
   A. P
   B. R
   C. S
   D. T
   E. None of the above. Sentence Q is last.

3. Which sentence did you put before Sentence T?
   A. P
   B. Q
   C. R
   D. S
   E. None of the above. Sentence T is last.

4. Which sentence did you put after Sentence R?
   A. P
   B. Q
   C. S
   D. T
   E. None of the above. Sentence R is last.

5. Which sentence did you put before Sentence R? 5.____
   A. P
   B. Q
   C. S
   D. T
   E. None of the above. Sentence R is first.

KEY (CORRECT ANSWERS)

1. D
2. E
3. A
4. B
5. D

TEST 5

DIRECTIONS: Each group of sentences in this section is actually a paragraph presented in scrambled order. Each sentence in the group has a place in that paragraph; no sentence is to be left out. You are to read each group of sentences so as to form a well-organized paragraph. Before trying to answer the questions which follow each group of sentences, jot down the correct order of the sentences. Then answer each of the questions by printing the letter of the correct answer in the space at the right. Remember that you will receive credit only for answers marked.

P. A *megagram*, or a million *grams*, is, therefore, equal to 2.205 pounds.
Q. A *gram* is equivalent to 1/28.35 ounces.
R. The fundamental unit of mass in the metric system is the *gram*.
S. A *kilogram*, or a thousand *grams*, is equal to 2.205 pounds.
T. *Gram* is derived from the late Greek, *gramma*, meaning a *small weight*.

1. Which sentence did you put after Sentence S?
   A. P
   B. Q
   C. R
   D. T
   E. None of the above. Sentence S is last.

2. Which sentence did you put before Sentence T?
   A. P
   B. Q
   C. R
   D. S
   E. None of the above. Sentence T is first.

3. Which sentence did you put after Sentence Q?
   A. P
   B. R
   C. S
   D. T
   E. None of the above. Sentence Q is last.

4. Which sentence did you put before Sentence R?
   A. P
   B. Q
   C. S
   D. T
   E. None of the above. Sentence R is first.

2 (#5)

5. Which sentence did you put after Sentence T? 5.____
    A. P
    B. Q
    C. R
    D. S
    E. None of the above. Sentence T is last.

KEY (CORRECT ANSWERS)

1. A
2. C
3. C
4. E
5. B

EXAMINATION SECTION
TEST 1

DIRECTIONS: Each group of sentences in this section is actually a paragraph presented in scrambled order. Each sentence in the group has a place in that paragraph; no sentence is to be left out. You are to read each group of sentences so as to form a well-organized paragraph. Before trying to answer the questions which follow each group of sentences, jot down the correct order of the sentences. Then answer each of the questions by printing the letter of the correct answer in the space at the right. Remember that you will receive credit only for answers marked.

P. Every man is a piece of the continent, a part of the main.
Q. So any man's death diminishes me, because I am involved in mankind. .
R. And, therefore, never send to know for whom the bell tolls; it tolls for thee.
S. No man is an island, entire of itself.
T. If a clod be washed away by the sea, Europe is the less.

1. Which sentence did you put before Sentence Q?

   A. P
   B. R
   C. S
   D. T
   E. None of the above. Sentence Q is first.

2. Which sentence did you put after Sentence S?

   A. P
   B. Q
   C. R
   D. T
   E. None of the above. Sentence S is last.

3. Which sentence did you put after Sentence R?

   A. P
   B. Q
   C. S
   D. T
   E. None of the above. Sentence R is last.

4. Which sentence did you put first?
   A. P   B. Q   C. R   D. S   E. T

5. Which sentence did you put before Sentence R?

   A. P
   B. Q
   C. S
   D. T
   E. None of the above. Sentence R is first.

KEY (CORRECT ANSWERS)

1. D
2. A
3. E
4. D
5. B

TEST 2

DIRECTIONS: Each group of sentences in this section is actually a paragraph presented in scrambled order. Each sentence in the group has a place in that paragraph; no sentence is to be left out. You are to read each group of sentences so as to form a well-organized paragraph. Before trying to answer the questions which follow each group of sentences, jot down the correct order of the sentences. Then answer each of the questions by printing the letter of the correct answer in the space at the right. Remember that you will receive credit only for answers marked.

P. Its glory is all moonshine.
Q. War is hell.
R. It is only they who seek more vengeance, more desolations.
S. I am sick and tired of war.
T. It is only those who have neither fired a shot nor heard the groans of the wounded who cry aloud for blood.

1. Which sentence did you put after Sentence T?   1.____

   A. P
   B. Q
   C. R
   D. S
   E. None of the above. Sentence T is last.

2. Which sentence did you put after Sentence P?   2.____

   A. Q
   B. R
   C. S
   D. T
   E. None of the above. Sentence P is last.

3. Which sentence did you put before Sentence S?   3.____

   A. P
   B. Q
   C. R
   D. T
   E. None of the above. Sentence S is first.

4. Which sentence did you put second?   4.____
   A. P   B. Q   C. R   D. S   E. T

5. Which sentence did you put first?   5.____
   A. P   B. Q   C. R   D. S   E. T

KEY (CORRECT ANSWERS)

1. C
2. D
3. E
4. A
5. D

TEST 3

DIRECTIONS: Each group of sentences in this section is actually a paragraph presented in scrambled order. Each sentence in the group has a place in that paragraph; no sentence is to be left out. You are to read each group of sentences so as to form a well-organized paragraph. Before trying to answer the questions which follow each group of sentences, jot down the correct order of the sentences. Then answer each of the questions by printing the letter of the correct answer in the space at the right. Remember that you will receive credit only for answers marked.

P. *Give crowns and pounds and guineas, but not your heart away.*
Q. *But keep your fancy free.*
R. But I was one-and-twenty; no use to talk to me.
S. When I was one-and-twenty, I heard a wise man say.
T. *Give pearls away and rubies.*

1. Which sentence did you put after Sentence Q?

   A. P
   B. R
   C. S
   D. T
   E. None of the above. Sentence Q is last.

2. Which sentence did you put first?

   A. P B. Q C. R D. S E. T

3. Which sentence did you put after Sentence T?

   A. P
   B. Q
   C. R
   D. S
   E. None of the above. Sentence T is last.

4. Which sentence did you put last?

   A. P B. Q C. R D. S E. T

5. Which sentence did you put before Sentence S?

   A. P
   B. Q
   C. R
   D. T
   E. None of the above. Sentence S is first.

KEY (CORRECT ANSWERS)

1. B
2. D
3. B
4. C
5. E

TEST 4

DIRECTIONS: Each group of sentences in this section is actually a paragraph presented in scrambled order. Each sentence in the group has a place in that paragraph; no sentence is to be left out. You are to read each group of sentences so as to form a well-organized paragraph. Before trying to answer the questions which follow each group of sentences, jot down the correct order of the sentences. Then answer each of the questions by printing the letter of the correct answer in the space at the right. Remember that you will receive credit only for answers marked.

P. But the problem is not only that of discipline in a particular art but of discipline in one's whole life.
Q. The practice of any art requires discipline.
R. When he does not work, he ordinarily wishes only to be lazy, to relax.
S. Yet modern man has exceedingly little self-discipline outside of the sphere of his work.
T. I shall never become expert at anything if I do not do it in a disciplined way.

1. Which sentence did you put after Sentence P?

   A. Q
   B. R
   C. S
   D. T
   E. None of the above. Sentence P is last.

2. Which sentence did you put before Sentence T?

   A. P
   B. Q
   C. R
   D. S
   E. None of the above. Sentence T is first.

3. Which sentence did you put last?
   A. P   B. Q   C. R   D. S   E. T

4. Which sentence did you put before Sentence P?

   A. Q
   B. R
   C. S
   D. T
   E. None of the above. Sentence P is first.

5. Which sentence did you put before Sentence Q?

   A. P
   B. R
   C. S
   D. T
   E. None of the above. Sentence Q is first.

KEY (CORRECT ANSWERS)

1. C
2. B
3. C
4. D
5. E

TEST 5

DIRECTIONS: Each group of sentences in this section is actually a paragraph presented in scrambled order. Each sentence in the group has a place in that paragraph; no sentence is to be left out. You are to read each group of sentences so as to form a well-organized paragraph. Before trying to answer the questions which follow each group of sentences, jot down the correct order of the sentences. Then answer each of the questions by printing the letter of the correct answer in the space at the right. Remember that you will receive credit only for answers marked.

P. That is, whoever insists on safety and security as primary conditions of life, cannot have faith.
Q. Love requires the courage to judge certain values as of ultimate.
R. To have faith requires courage.
S. The courage that faith and love require is not, however, nerely *living dangerously,* which is the courage of nihilism.
T. To be loved, to love, also require courage.

1. Which sentence did you put third?

   A. P   B. Q   C. R   D. S   E. T

2. Which sentence did you put before Sentence P?

   A. Q
   B. R
   C. S
   D. T
   E. None of the above. Sentence P is first.

3. Which sentence did you put after Sentence S?

   A. P
   B. Q
   C. R
   D. T
   E. None of the above. Sentence S is last.

4. Which sentence did you put before Sentence S?

   A. P
   B. Q
   C. R
   D. T
   E. None of the above. Sentence S is first.

5. Which sentence did you put first?

   A. P   B. Q   C. R   D. S   E. T

KEY (CORRECT ANSWERS)

1. E
2. B
3. E
4. B
5. C

PHILOSOPHY, PRINCIPLES, PRACTICES, AND TECHNICS
OF
SUPERVISION, ADMINISTRATION, MANAGEMENT, AND ORGANIZATION

TABLE OF CONTENTS

	Page
MEANING OF SUPERVISION	1
THE OLD AND THE NEW SUPERVISION	1
THE EIGHT (8) BASIC PRINCIPLES OF THE NEW SUPERVISION	1
I. Principle of Responsibility	1
II. Principle of Authority	2
III. Principle of Self-Growth	2
IV. Principle of Individual Worth	2
V. Principle of Creative Leadership	2
VI. Principle of Success and Failure	2
VII. Principle of Science	3
VIII. Principle of Cooperation	3
WHAT IS ADMINISTRATION?	3
I. Practices Commonly Classed as "Supervisory"	3
II. Practices Commonly Classed as "Administrative"	3
III. Practices Commonly Classed as Both "Supervisory" and "Administrative"	4
RESPONSIBILITIES OF THE SUPERVISOR	4
COMPETENCIES OF THE SUPERVISOR	4
THE PROFESSIONAL SUPERVISOR-EMPLOYEE RELATIONSHIP	4
MINI-TEXT IN SUPERVISION, ADMINISTRATION, MANAGEMENT, AND ORGANIZATION	5
I. Brief Highlights	5
A. Levels of Management	6
B. What the Supervisor Must Learn	6
C. A Definition of Supervision	6
D. Elements of the Team Concept	6
E. Principles of Organization	6
F. The Four Important Parts of Every Job	7
G. Principles of Delegation	7
H. Principles of Effective Communications	7
I. Principles of Work Improvement	7
J. Areas of Job Improvement	7
K. Seven Key Points in Making Improvements	8

	L.	Corrective Techniques for Job Improvement	8
	M.	A Planning Checklist	8
	N.	Five Characteristics of Good Directions	9
	O.	Types of Directions	9
	P.	Controls	9
	Q.	Orienting the New Employee	9
	R.	Checklist for Orienting New Employees	9
	S.	Principles of Learning	10
	T.	Causes of Poor Performance	10
	U.	Four Major Steps in On-the-Job Instructions	10
	V.	Employees Want Five Things	10
	W.	Some Don'ts in Regard to Praise	11
	X.	How to Gain Your Workers' Confidence	11
	Y.	Sources of Employee Problems	11
	Z.	The Supervisor's Key to Discipline	11
	AA.	Five Important Processes of Management	12
	BB.	When the Supervisor Fails to Plan	12
	CC.	Fourteen General Principles of Management	12
	DD.	Change	12
II.	Brief Topical Summaries		13
	A.	Who/What is the Supervisor?	13
	B.	The Sociology of Work	13
	C.	Principles and Practices of Supervision	14
	D.	Dynamic Leadership	14
	E.	Processes for Solving Problems	15
	F.	Training for Results	15
	G.	Health, Safety, and Accident Prevention	16
	H.	Equal Employment Opportunity	16
	I.	Improving Communications	16
	J.	Self-Development	17
	K.	Teaching and Training	17
		1. The Teaching Process	17
		a. Preparation	17
		b. Presentation	18
		c. Summary	18
		d. Application	18
		e. Evaluation	18
		2. Teaching Methods	18
		a. Lecture	18
		b. Discussion	18
		c. Demonstration	19
		d. Performance	19
		e. Which Method to Use	19

PHILOSOPHY, PRINCIPLES, PRACTICES, AND TECHNICS
OF
SUPERVISION, ADMINISTRATION, MANAGEMENT, AND ORGANIZATION

MEANING OF SUPERVISION

The extension of the democratic philosophy has been accompanied by an extension in the scope of supervision. Modern leaders and supervisors no longer think of supervision in the narrow sense of being confined chiefly to visiting employees, supplying materials, or rating the staff. They regard supervision as being intimately related to all the concerned agencies of society, they speak of the supervisor's function in terms of "growth," rather than the "improvement" of employees.

This modern concept of supervision may be defined as follows: Supervision is leadership and the development of leadership within groups which are cooperatively engaged in inspection, research, training, guidance, and evaluation.

THE OLD AND THE NEW SUPERVISION

TRADITIONAL
1. Inspection
2. Focused on the employee
3. Visitation
4. Random and haphazard
5. Imposed and authoritarian
6. One person usually

MODERN
1. Study and analysis
2. Focused on aims, materials, methods, supervisors, employees, environment
3. Demonstrations, intervisitation, workshops, directed reading, bulletins, etc.
4. Definitely organized and planned (scientific)
5. Cooperative and democratic
6. Many persons involved (creative)

THE EIGHT (8) BASIC PRINCIPLES OF THE NEW SUPERVISION

I. Principle of Responsibility
Authority to act and responsibility for acting must be joined.
A. If you give responsibility, give authority.
B. Define employee duties clearly.
C. Protect employees from criticism by others.
D. Recognize the rights as well as obligations of employees.
E. Achieve the aims of a democratic society insofar as it is possible within the area of your work.
F. Establish a situation favorable to training and learning.
G. Accept ultimate responsibility for everything done in your section, unit, office, division, department.
H. Good administration and good supervision are inseparable.

II. Principle of Authority
The success of the supervisor is measured by the extent to which the power of authority is not used.
   A. Exercise simplicity and informality in supervision
   B. Use the simplest machinery of supervision
   C. If it is good for the organization as a whole, it is probably justified.
   D. Seldom be arbitrary or authoritative.
   E. Do not base your work on the power of position or of personality.
   F. Permit and encourage the free expression of opinions.

III. Principle of Self-Growth
The success of the supervisor is measured by the extent to which, and the speed with which, he is no longer needed.
   A. Base criticism on principles, not on specifics.
   B. Point out higher activities to employees.
   C. Train for self-thinking by employees to meet new situations.
   D. Stimulate initiative, self-reliance, and individual responsibility
   E. Concentrate on stimulating the growth of employees rather than on removing defects.

IV. Principle of Individual Worth
Respect for the individual is a paramount consideration in supervision.
   A. Be human and sympathetic in dealing with employees.
   B. Don't nag about things to be done.
   C. Recognize the individual differences among employees and seek opportunities to permit best expression of each personality.

V. Principle of Creative Leadership
The best supervision is that which is not apparent to the employee.
   A. Stimulate, don't drive employees to creative action.
   B. Emphasize doing good things.
   C. Encourage employees to do what they do best.
   D. Do not be too greatly concerned with details of subject or method.
   E. Do not be concerned exclusively with immediate problems and activities.
   F. Reveal higher activities and make them both desired and maximally possible.
   G. Determine procedures in the light of each situation but see that these are derived from a sound basic philosophy.
   H. Aid, inspire, and lead so as to liberate the creative spirit latent in all good employees.

VI. Principle of Success and Failure
There are no unsuccessful employees, only unsuccessful supervisors who have failed to give proper leadership.
   A. Adapt suggestions to the capacities, attitudes, and prejudices of employees.
   B. Be gradual, be progressive, be persistent.
   C. Help the employee find the general principle; have the employee apply his own problem to the general principle.
   D. Give adequate appreciation for good work and honest effort.
   E. Anticipate employee difficulties and help to prevent them.
   F. Encourage employees to do the desirable things they will do anyway.
   G. Judge your supervision by the results it secures.

VII. Principle of Science
Successful supervision is scientific, objective, and experimental. It is based on facts, not on prejudices.
   A. Be cumulative in results.
   B. Never divorce your suggestions from the goals of training.
   C. Don't be impatient of results.
   D. Keep all matters on a professional, not a personal, level.
   E. Do not be concerned exclusively with immediate problems and activities.
   F. Use objective means of determining achievement and rating where possible.

VIII. Principle of Cooperation
Supervision is a cooperative enterprise between supervisor and employee.
   A. Begin with conditions as they are.
   B. Ask opinions of all involved when formulating policies.
   C. Organization is as good as its weakest link.
   D. Let employees help to determine policies and department programs.
   E. Be approachable and accessible—physically and mentally.
   F. Develop pleasant social relationships.

WHAT IS ADMINISTRATION

Administration is concerned with providing the environment, the material facilities, and the operational procedures that will promote the maximum growth and development of supervisors and employees. (Organization is an aspect and a concomitant of administration.)

There is no sharp line of demarcation between supervision and administration; these functions are intimately interrelated and, often, overlapping. They are complementary activities.

I. Practices Commonly Classed as "Supervisory"
   A. Conducting employees' conferences
   B. Visiting sections, units, offices, divisions, departments
   C. Arranging for demonstrations
   D. Examining plans
   E. Suggesting professional reading
   F. Interpreting bulletins
   G. Recommending in-service training courses
   H. Encouraging experimentation
   I. Appraising employee morale
   J. Providing for intervisitation

II. Practices Commonly Classified as "Administrative"
   A. Management of the office
   B. Arrangement of schedules for extra duties
   C. Assignment of rooms or areas
   D. Distribution of supplies
   E. Keeping records and reports
   F. Care of audio-visual materials
   G. Keeping inventory records
   H. Checking record cards and books

I. Programming special activities
J. Checking on the attendance and punctuality of employees

III. Practices Commonly Classified as Both "Supervisory" and "Administrative"
   A. Program construction
   B. Testing or evaluating outcomes
   C. Personnel accounting
   D. Ordering instructional materials

RESPONSIBILITIES OF THE SUPERVISOR

A person employed in a supervisory capacity must constantly be able to improve his own efficiency and ability. He represent the employer to the employees and only continuous self-examination can make him a capable supervisor.

Leadership and training are the supervisor's responsibility. An efficient working unit is one in which the employees work with the supervisor. It is his job to bring out the best in his employees. He must always be relaxed, courteous, and calm in his association with his employees. Their feelings are important, and a harsh attitude does not develop the most efficient employees.

COMPETENCES OF THE SUPERVISOR

I. Complete knowledge of the duties and responsibilities of his position.
II. To be able to organize a job, plan ahead, and carry through.
III. To have self-confidence and initiative.
IV. To be able to handle the unexpected situation and make quick decisions.
V. To be able to properly train subordinates in the positions they are best suited for.
VI. To be able to keep good human relations among his subordinates.
VII. To be able to keep good human relations between his subordinates and himself and to earn their respect and trust.

THE PROFESSIONAL SUPERVISOR-EMPLOYEE RELATIONSHIP

There are two kinds of efficiency: one kind is only apparent and is produced in organizations through the exercise of mere discipline; this is but a simulation of the second, or true, efficiency which springs from spontaneous cooperation. If you are a manager, no matter how great or small your responsibility, it is your job, in the final analysis, to create and develop this involuntary cooperation among the people whom you supervise. For, no matter how powerful a combination of money, machines, and materials a company may have, this is a dead and sterile thing without a team of willing, thinking, and articulate people to guide it.

The following 21 points are presented as indicative of the exemplary basic relationship that should exist between supervisor and employee:

1. Each person wants to be liked and respected by his fellow employee and wants to be treated with consideration and respect by his superior.
2. The most competent employee will make an error. However, in a unit where good relations exist between the supervisor and his employees, tenseness and fear do not exist. Thus, errors are not hidden or covered up, and the efficiency of a unit is not impaired.

3. Subordinates resent rules, regulations, or orders that are unreasonable or unexplained.
4. Subordinates are quick to resent unfairness, harshness, injustices, and favoritism.
5. An employee will accept responsibility if he knows that he will be complimented for a job well done, and not too harshly chastised for failure; that his supervisor will check the cause of the failure, and, if it was the supervisor's fault, he will assume the blame therefore. If it was the employee's fault, his supervisor will explain the correct method or means of handling the responsibility.
6. An employee wants to receive credit for a suggestion he has made, that is used. If a suggestion cannot be used, the employee is entitled to an explanation. The supervisor should not say "no" and close the subject.
7. Fear and worry slow up a worker's ability. Poor working environment can impair his physical and mental health. A good supervisor avoids forceful methods, threats, and arguments to get a job done.
8. A forceful supervisor is able to train his employees individually and as a team, and is able to motivate them in the proper channels.
9. A mature supervisor is able to properly evaluate his subordinates and to keep them happy and satisfied.
10. A sensitive supervisor will never patronize his subordinates.
11. A worthy supervisor will respect his employees' confidences.
12. Definite and clear-cut responsibilities should be assigned to each executive.
13. Responsibility should always be coupled with corresponding authority.
14. No change should be made in the scope or responsibilities of a position without a definite understanding to that effect on the part of all persons concerned.
15. No executive or employee, occupying a single position in the organization, should be subject to definite orders from more than one source.
16. Orders should never be given to subordinates over the head of a responsible executive. Rather than do this, the officer in question should be supplanted.
17. Criticisms of subordinates should, whoever possible, be made privately, and in no case should a subordinate be criticized in the presence of executives or employees of equal or lower rank.
18. No dispute or difference between executives or employees as to authority or responsibilities should be considered too trivial for prompt and careful adjudication.
19. Promotions, wage changes, and disciplinary action should always be approved by the executive immediately superior to the one directly responsible.
20. No executive or employee should ever be required, or expected, to be at the same time an assistant to, and critic of, another.
21. Any executive whose work is subject to regular inspection should, wherever practicable, be given the assistance and facilities necessary to enable him to maintain an independent check of the quality of his work.

MINI-TEXT IN SUPERVISION, ADMINISTRATION, MANAGEMENT, AND ORGANIZATION

I. Brief Highlights

Listed concisely and sequentially are major headings and important data in the field for quick recall and review.

A. Levels of Management
Any organization of some size has several levels of management. In terms of a ladder, the levels are:

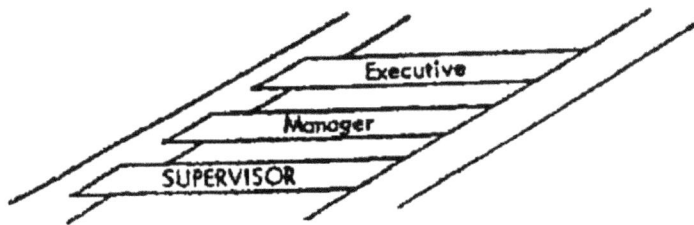

The first level is very important because it is the beginning point of management leadership.

B. What the Supervisor Must Learn
A supervisor must learn to:
1. Deal with people and their differences
2. Get the job done through people
3. Recognize the problems when they exist
4. Overcome obstacles to good performance
5. Evaluate the performance of people
6. Check his own performance in terms of accomplishment

C. A Definition of Supervisor
The term supervisor means any individual having authority, in the interests of the employer, to hire, transfer, suspend, lay-off, recall, promote, discharge, assign, reward, or discipline other employees or responsibility to direct them, or to adjust their grievances, or effectively to recommend such action, if, in connection with the foregoing, exercise of such authority is not of a merely routine or clerical nature but requires the use of independent judgment.

D. Elements of the Team Concept
What is involved in teamwork? The component parts are:
1. Members
2. A leader
3. Goals
4. Plans
5. Cooperation
6. Spirit

E. Principles of Organization
1. A team member must know what his job is.
2. Be sure that the nature and scope of a job are understood.
3. Authority and responsibility should be carefully spelled out.
4. A supervisor should be permitted to make the maximum number of decisions affecting his employees.
5. Employees should report to only one supervisor.
6. A supervisor should direct only as many employees as he can handle effectively.
7. An organization plan should be flexible.

8. Inspection and performance of work should be separate.
9. Organizational problems should receive immediate attention.
10. Assign work in line with ability and experience.

F. The Four Important Parts of Every Job
   1. Inherent in every job is the *accountability* for results.
   2. A second set of factors in every job is *responsibilities*.
   3. Along with duties and responsibilities one must have the *authority* to act within certain limits without obtaining permission to proceed.
   4. No job exists in a vacuum. The supervisor is surrounded by key *relationships*.

G. Principles of Delegation
   Where work is delegated for the first time, the supervisor should think in terms of these questions:
   1. Who is best qualified to do this?
   2. Can an employee improve his abilities by doing this?
   3. How long should an employee spend on this?
   4. Are there any special problems for which he will need guidance?
   5. How broad a delegation can I make?

H. Principles of Effective Communications
   1. Determine the media.
   2. To whom directed?
   3. Identification and source authority.
   4. Is communication understood?

I. Principles of Work Improvement
   1. Most people usually do only the work which is assigned to them.
   2. Workers are likely to fit assigned work into the time available to perform it.
   3. A good workload usually stimulates output.
   4. People usually do their best work when they know that results will be reviewed or inspected.
   5. Employees usually feel that someone else is responsible for conditions of work, workplace layout, job methods, type of tools/equipment, and other such factors.
   6. Employees are usually defensive about their job security.
   7. Employees have natural resistance to change.
   8. Employees can support or destroy a supervisor.
   9. A supervisor usually earns the respect of his people through his personal example of diligence and efficiency.

J. Areas of Job Improvement
   The areas of job improvement are quite numerous, but the most common ones which a supervisor can identify and utilize are:
   1. Departmental layout
   2. Flow of work
   3. Workplace layout
   4. Utilization of manpower
   5. Work methods
   6. Materials handling

7. Utilization
8. Motion economy

K. Seven Key Points in Making Improvements
1. Select the job to be improved
2. Study how it is being done now
3. Question the present method
4. Determine actions to be taken
5. Chart proposed method
6. Get approval and apply
7. Solicit worker participation

l. Corrective Techniques of Job Improvement
Specific Problems
1. Size of workload
2. Inability to meet schedules
3. Strain and fatigue
4. Improper use of men and skills
5. Waste, poor quality, unsafe conditions
6. Bottleneck conditions that hinder output
7. Poor utilization of equipment and machine
8. Efficiency and productivity of labor

General Improvement
1. Departmental layout
2. Flow of work
3. Work plan layout
4. Utilization of manpower
5. Work methods
6. Materials handling
7. Utilization of equipment
8. Motion economy

Corrective Techniques
1. Study with scale model
2. Flow chart study
3. Motion analysis
4. Comparison of units produced to standard allowance
5. Methods analysis
6. Flow chart and equipment study
7. Down time vs. running time
8. Motion analysis

M. A Planning Checklist
1. Objectives
2. Controls
3. Delegations
4. Communications
5. Resources
6. Manpower

7. Equipment
8. Supplies and materials
9. Utilization of time
10. Safety
11. Money
12. Work
13. Timing of improvements

N. Five Characteristics of Good Directions
In order to get results, directions must be:
1. Possible of accomplishment
2. Agreeable with worker interests
3. Related to mission
4. Planned and complete
5. Unmistakably clear

O. Types of Directions
1. Demands or direct orders
2. Requests
3. Suggestion or implication
4. volunteering

P. Controls
A typical listing of the overall areas in which the supervisor should establish controls might be:
1. Manpower
2. Materials
3. Quality of work
4. Quantity of work
5. Time
6. Space
7. Money
8. Methods

Q. Orienting the New Employee
1. Prepare for him
2. Welcome the new employee
3. Orientation for the job
4. Follow-up

R. Checklist for Orienting New Employees   Yes   No
1. Do you appreciate the feelings of new employees
   when they first report for work?   ___   ___
2. Are you aware of the fact that the new employee must
   make a big adjustment to his job?   ___   ___
3. Have you given him good reasons for liking the job and
   the organization?   ___   ___
4. Have you prepared for his first day on the job?   ___   ___
5. Did you welcome him cordially and make him feel needed?   ___   ___

	Yes	No

6. Did you establish rapport with him so that he feels free to talk and discuss matters with you? ___ ___
7. Did you explain his job to him and his relationship to you? ___ ___
8. Does he know that his work will be evaluated periodically on a basis that is fair and objective? ___ ___
9. Did you introduce him to his fellow workers in such a way that they are likely to accept him? ___ ___
10. Does he know what employee benefits he will receive? ___ ___
11. Does he understand the importance of being on the job and what to do if he must leave his duty station? ___ ___
12. Has he been impressed with the importance of accident prevention and safe practice? ___ ___
13. Does he generally know his way around the department? ___ ___
14. Is he under the guidance of a sponsor who will teach the right way of doing things? ___ ___
15. Do you plan to follow-up so that he will continue to adjust successfully to his job? ___ ___

S. Principles of Learning
 1. Motivation
 2. Demonstration or explanation
 3. Practice

T. Causes of Poor Performance
 1. Improper training for job
 2. Wrong tools
 3. Inadequate directions
 4. Lack of supervisory follow-up
 5. Poor communications
 6. Lack of standards of performance
 7. Wrong work habits
 8. Low morale
 9. Other

U. Four Major Steps in On-The-Job Instruction
 1. Prepare the worker
 2. Present the operation
 3. Tryout performance
 4. Follow-up

V. Employees Want Five Things
 1. Security
 2. Opportunity
 3. Recognition
 4. Inclusion
 5. Expression

W. Some Don'ts in Regard to Praise
1. Don't praise a person for something he hasn't done.
2. Don't praise a person unless you can be sincere.
3. Don't be sparing in praise just because your superior withholds it from you.
4. Don't let too much time elapse between good performance and recognition of it

X. How to Gain Your Workers' Confidence
Methods of developing confidence include such things as:
1. Knowing the interests, habits, hobbies of employees
2. Admitting your own inadequacies
3. Sharing and telling of confidence in others
4. Supporting people when they are in trouble
5. Delegating matters that can be well handled
6. Being frank and straightforward about problems and working conditions
7. Encouraging others to bring their problems to you
8. Taking action on problems which impede worker progress

Y. Sources of Employee Problems
On-the-job causes might be such things as:
1. A feeling that favoritism is exercised in assignments
2. Assignment of overtime
3. An undue amount of supervision
4. Changing methods or systems
5. Stealing of ideas or trade secrets
6. Lack of interest in job
7. Threat of reduction in force
8. Ignorance or lack of communications
9. Poor equipment
10. Lack of knowing how supervisor feels toward employee
11. Shift assignments

Off-the-job problems might have to do with:
1. Health
2. Finances
3. Housing
4. Family

Z. The Supervisor's Key to Discipline
There are several key points about discipline which the supervisor should keep in mind:
1. Job discipline is one of the disciplines of life and is directed by the supervisor.
2. It is more important to correct an employee fault than to fix blame for it.
3. Employee performance is affected by problems both on the job and off.
4. Sudden or abrupt changes in behavior can be indications of important employee problems.
5. Problems should be dealt with as soon as possible after they are identified.
6. The attitude of the supervisor may have more to do with solving problems than the techniques of problem solving.
7. Correction of employee behavior should be resorted to only after the supervisor is sure that training or counseling will not be helpful.

8. Be sure to document your disciplinary actions.
9. Make sure that you are disciplining on the basis of facts rather than personal feelings.
10. Take each disciplinary step in order, being careful not to make snap judgments, or decisions based on impatience.

AA. Five Important Processes of Management
1. Planning
2. Organizing
3. Scheduling
4. Controlling
5. Motivating

BB. When the Supervisor Fails to Plan
1. Supervisor creates impression of not knowing his job
2. May lead to excessive overtime
3. Job runs itself—supervisor lacks control
4. Deadlines and appointments missed
5. Parts of the work go undone
6. Work interrupted by emergencies
7. Sets a bad example
8. Uneven workload creates peaks and valleys
9. Too much time on minor details at expense of more important tasks

CC. Fourteen General Principles of Management
1. Division of work
2. Authority and responsibility
3. Discipline
4. Unity of command
5. Unity of direction
6. Subordination of individual interest to general interest
7. Remuneration of personnel
8. Centralization
9. Scalar chain
10. Order
11. Equity
12. Stability of tenure of personnel
13. Initiative
14. Esprit de corps

DD. Change

Bringing about change is perhaps attempted more often, and yet less well understood, than anything else the supervisor does. How do people generally react to change? (People tend to resist change that is imposed upon them by other individuals or circumstances.

Change is characteristic of every situation. It is a part of every real endeavor where the efforts of people are concerned.

1. Why do people resist change?
   People may resist change because of:
   a. Fear of the unknown
   b. Implied criticism
   c. Unpleasant experiences in the past
   d. Fear of loss of status
   e. Threat to the ego
   f. Fear of loss of economic stability

2. How can we best overcome the resistance to change?
   In initiating change, take these steps:
   a. Get ready to sell
   b. Identify sources of help
   c. Anticipate objections
   d. Sell benefits
   e. Listen in depth
   f. Follow up

II. Brief Topical Summaries

   A. Who/What is the Supervisor?
      1. The supervisor is often called the "highest level employee and the lowest level manager."
      2. A supervisor is a member of both management and the work group. He acts as a bridge between the two.
      3. Most problems in supervision are in the area of human relations, or people problems.
      4. Employees expect: Respect, opportunity to learn and to advance, and a sense of belonging, and so forth.
      5. Supervisors are responsible for directing people and organizing work. Planning is of paramount importance.
      6. A position description is a set of duties and responsibilities inherent to a given position.
      7. It is important to keep the position description up-to-date and to provide each employee with his own copy.

   B. The Sociology of Work
      1. People are alike in many ways; however, each individual is unique.
      2. The supervisor is challenged in getting to know employee differences. Acquiring skills in evaluating individuals is an asset.
      3. Maintaining meaningful working relationships in the organization is of great importance.
      4. The supervisor has an obligation to help individuals to develop to their fullest potential.
      5. Job rotation on a planned basis helps to build versatility and to maintain interest and enthusiasm in work groups.
      6. Cross training (job rotation) provides backup skills.

7. The supervisor can help reduce tension by maintaining a sense of humor, providing guidance to employees, and by making reasonable and timely decisions. Employees respond favorably to working under reasonably predictable circumstances.
8. Change is characteristic of all managerial behavior. The supervisor must adjust to changes in procedures, new methods, technological changes, and to a number of new and sometimes challenging situations.
9. To overcome the natural tendency for people to resist change, the supervisor should become more skillful in initiating change.

C. Principles and Practices of Supervision
1. Employees should be required to answer to only one superior.
2. A supervisor can effectively direct only a limited number of employees, depending upon the complexity, variety, and proximity of the jobs involved.
3. The organizational chart presents the organization in graphic form. It reflects lines of authority and responsibility as well as interrelationships of units within the organization.
4. Distribution of work can be improved through an analysis using the "Work Distribution Chart."
5. The "Work Distribution Chart" reflects the division of work within a unit in understandable form.
6. When related tasks are given to an employee, he has a better chance of increasing his skills through training.
7. The individual who is given the responsibility for tasks must also be given the appropriate authority to insure adequate results.
8. The supervisor should delegate repetitive, routine work. Preparation of recurring reports, maintaining leave and attendance records are some examples.
9. Good discipline is essential to good task performance. Discipline is reflected in the actions of employees on the job in the absence of supervision.
10. Disciplinary action may have to be taken when the positive aspects of discipline have failed. Reprimand, warning, and suspension are examples of disciplinary action.
11. If a situation calls for a reprimand, be sure it is deserved and remember it is to be done in private.

D. Dynamic Leadership
1. A style is a personal method or manner of exerting influence.
2. Authoritarian leaders often see themselves as the source of power and authority.
3. The democratic leader often perceives the group as the source of authority and power.
4. Supervisors tend to do better when using the pattern of leadership that is most natural for them.
5. Social scientists suggest that the effective supervisor use the leadership style that best fits the problem or circumstances involved.
6. All four styles—telling, selling, consulting, joining—have their place. Using one does not preclude using the other at another time.

7. The theory X point of view assumes that the average person dislikes work, will avoid it whenever possible, and must be coerced to achieve organizational objectives.
8. The theory Y point of view assumes that the average person considers work to be a natural as play, and, when the individual is committed, he requires little supervision or direction to accomplish desired objectives.
9. The leader's basic assumptions concerning human behavior and human nature affect his actions, decisions, and other managerial practices.
10. Dissatisfaction among employees is often present, but difficult to isolate. The supervisor should seek to weaken dissatisfaction by keeping promises, being sincere and considerate, keeping employees informed, and so forth.
11. Constructive suggestions should be encouraged during the natural progress of the work.

E. Processes for Solving Problems
1. People find their daily tasks more meaningful and satisfying when they can improve them.
2. The causes of problems, or the key factors, are often hidden in the background. Ability to solve problems often involves the ability to isolate them from their backgrounds. There is some substance to the cliché that some persons "can't see the forest for the trees."
3. New procedures are often developed from old ones. Problems should be broken down into manageable parts. New ideas can be adapted from old one.
4. People think differently in problem-solving situations. Using a logical, patterned approach is often useful. One approach found to be useful includes these steps:
   a. Define the problem
   b. Establish objectives
   c. Get the facts
   d. Weigh and decide
   e. Take action
   f. Evaluate action

F. Training for Results
1. Participants respond best when they feel training is important to them.
2. The supervisor has responsibility for the training and development of those who report to him.
3. When training is delegated to others, great care must be exercised to insure the trainer has knowledge, aptitude, and interest for his work as a trainer.
4. Training (learning) of some type goes on continually. The most successful supervisor makes certain the learning contributes in a productive manner to operational goals.
5. New employees are particularly susceptible to training. Older employees facing new job situations require specific training, as well as having need for development and growth opportunities.
6. Training needs require continuous monitoring.
7. The training officer of an agency is a professional with a responsibility to assist supervisors in solving training problems.

8. Many of the self-development steps important to the supervisor's own growth are equally important to the development of peers and subordinates. Knowledge of these is important when the supervisor consults with others on development and growth opportunities.

G. Health, Safety, and Accident Prevention
1. Management-minded supervisors take appropriate measures to assist employees in maintaining health and in assuring safe practices in the work environment.
2. Effective safety training and practices help to avoid injury and accidents.
3. Safety should be a management goal. All infractions of safety which are observed should be corrected without exception.
4. Employees' safety attitude, training and instruction, provision of safe tools and equipment, supervision, and leadership are considered highly important factors which contribute to safety and which can be influenced directly by supervisors.
5. When accidents do occur, they should be investigated promptly for very important reasons, including the fact that information which is gained can be used to prevent accidents in the future.

H. Equal Employment Opportunity
1. The supervisor should endeavor to treat all employees fairly, without regard to religion, race, sex, or national origin.
2. Groups tend to reflect the attitude of the leader. Prejudice can be detected even in very subtle form. Supervisors must strive to create a feeling of mutual respect and confidence in every employee.
3. Complete utilization of all human resources is a national goal. Equitable consideration should be accorded women in the work force, minority-group members, the physically and mentally handicapped, and the older employee. The important question is: "Who can do the job?"
4. Training opportunities, recognition for performance, overtime assignments, promotional opportunities, and all other personnel actions are to be handled on an equitable basis.

I. Improving Communications
1. Communications is achieving understanding between the sender and the receiver of a message. It also means sharing information—the creation of understanding.
2. Communication is basic to all human activity. Words are means of conveying meanings; however, real meanings are in people.
3. There are very practical differences in the effectiveness of one-way, impersonal, and two-way communications. Words spoken face-to-face are better understood. Telephone conversations are effective, but lack the rapport of person-to-person exchanges. The whole person communicates.
4. Cooperation and communication in an organization go hand in hand. When there is a mutual respect between people, spelling out rules and procedures for communicating is unnecessary.
5. There are several barriers to effective communications. These include failure to listen with respect and understanding, lack of skill in feedback, and misinterpreting the meanings of words used by the speaker. It is also common

practice to listen to what we want to hear, and tune out things we do not want to hear.
6. Communication is management's chief problem. The supervisor should accept the challenge to communicate more effectively and to improve interagency and intra-agency communications.
7. The supervisor may often plan for and conduct meetings. The planning phase is critical and may determine the success or the failure of a meeting.
8. Speaking before groups usually requires extra effort. Stage fright may never disappear completely, but it can be controlled.

J. Self-Development
1. Every employee is responsible for his own self-development.
2. Toastmaster and toastmistress clubs offer opportunities to improve skills in oral communications.
3. Planning for one's own self-development is of vital importance. Supervisors know their own strengths and limitations better than anyone else.
4. Many opportunities are open to aid the supervisor in his developmental efforts, including job assignments; training opportunities, both governmental and non-governmental—to include universities and professional conferences and seminars.
5. Programmed instruction offers a means of studying at one's own rate.
6. Where difficulties may arise from a supervisor's being away from his work for training, he may participate in televised home study or correspondence courses to meet his self-development needs.

K. Teaching and Training
1. The Teaching Process
Teaching is encouraging and guiding the learning activities of students toward established goals. In most cases this process consists of five steps: preparation, presentation, summarization, evaluation, and application.

   a. Preparation
   Preparation is two-fold in nature; that of the supervisor and the employee. Preparation by the supervisor is absolutely essential to success. He must know what, when, where, how, and whom he will teach. Some of the factors that should be considered are:
   1) The objectives
   2) The materials needed
   3) The methods to be used
   4) Employee participation
   5) Employee interest
   6) Training aids
   7) Evaluation
   8) Summarization

   Employee preparation consists in preparing the employee to receive the material. Probably the most important single factor in the preparation of the employee is arousing and maintaining his interest. He must know the objectives of the training, why he is there, how the material can be used, and its importance to him.

b. Presentation
In presentation, have a carefully designed plan and follow it. The plan should be accurate and complete, yet flexible enough to meet situations as they arise. The method of presentation will be determined by the particular situation and objectives.

c. Summary
A summary should be made at the end of every training unit and program. In addition, there may be internal summaries depending on the nature of the material being taught. The important thing is that the trainee must always be able to understand how each part of the new material relates to the whole.

d. Application
The supervisor must arrange work so the employee will be given a chance to apply new knowledge or skills while the material is still clear in his mind and interest is high. The trainee does not really know whether he has learned the material until he has been given a chance to apply it. If the material is not applied, it loses most of its value.

e. Evaluation
The purpose of all training is to promote learning. To determine whether the training has been a success or failure, the supervisor must evaluate this learning.
In the broadest sense, evaluation includes all the devices, methods, skills, and techniques used by the supervisor to keep himself and the employees informed as to their progress toward the objectives they are pursuing. The extent to which the employee has mastered the knowledge, skills, and abilities, or changed his attitudes, as determined by the program objectives, is the extent to which instruction has succeeded or failed.
Evaluation should not be confined to the end of the lesson, day, or program but should be used continuously. We shall note later the way this relates to the rest of the teaching process.

2. Teaching Methods
A teaching method is a pattern of identifiable student and instructor activity used in presenting training material.
All supervisors are faced with the problem of deciding which method should be used at a given time.

a. Lecture
The lecture is direct oral presentation of material by the supervisor. The present trend is to place less emphasis on the trainer's activity and more on that of the trainee.

b. Discussion
Teaching by discussion or conference involves using questions and other techniques to arouse interest and focus attention upon certain areas, and by doing so creating a learning situation. This can be one of the most

valuable methods because it gives the employees an opportunity to express their ideas and pool their knowledge.

c. Demonstration
The demonstration is used to teach how something works or how to do something. It can be used to show a principle or what the results of a series of actions will be. A well-staged demonstration is particularly effective because it shows proper methods of performance in a realistic manner.

d. Performance
Performance is one of the most fundamental of all learning techniques or teaching methods. The trainee may be able to tell how a specific operation should be performed but he cannot be sure he knows how to perform the operation until he has done so.
As with all methods, there are certain advantages and disadvantages to each method.

e. Which Method to Use
Moreover, there are other methods and techniques of teaching. It is difficult to use any method without other methods entering into it. In any learning situation, a combination of methods is usually more effective than any one method alone.

Finally, evaluation must be integrated into the other aspects of the teaching-learning process.

It must be used in the motivation of the trainees; it must be used to assist in developing understanding during the training; and it must be related to employee application of the results of training.

This is distinctly the role of the supervisor.

www.ingramcontent.com/pod-product-compliance
Lightning Source LLC
Chambersburg PA
CBHW081821300426
44116CB00014B/2440